Impossible
Realities

Impossible Realities

THE SCIENCE BEHIND ENERGY HEALING,
TELEPATHY, REINCARNATION, PRECOGNITION,
AND OTHER BLACK SWAN PHENOMENA

MAUREEN CAUDILL

HAMPTON ROADS

Cover design by Jim Warner
Interior designed by Maureen Forys, Happenstance Type-O-Rama

Hampton Roads Publishing Company, Inc.
Charlottesville, VA 22906
Distributed by Red Wheel/Weiser, LLC
www.redwheelweiser.com

Sign up for our newsletter and special offers by going to
www.redwheelweiser.com/newsletter/.

ISBN: 978-1-57174-663-4

Library of Congress Cataloging-in-Publication Data available upon request

Printed in Canada

FR

10 9 8 7 6 5 4 3 2 1

Dedicated to

Deb, Chief Nag-ivator Extraordinaire, for more reasons than I can possibly list,

and

Caro, who went out of her way to keep the Feline Manager happy with brushies, not to mention being an Errand Angel who went so far as to cook actual food in order to see to the care and feeding of a desperate writer when schedules got tight,

and of course,

Tinkerbell, Supreme Royal Feline Manager, whose careful supervision of writing sessions was an invaluable source of inspiration and encouragement, plus—just in case—thanks, Mom!

Contents

Acknowledgments

I would like to thank my excellent and kind editor, Caroline Pincus, whose wise advice I treasured. No book is the product of a single person. There is always a team of editors, publicists, cover artists, book designers, and many other people who change the author's raw manuscript into a professionally produced book. I would like to tip my hat to the team at Red Wheel/Weiser. Thank you all for your hard work!

Black Swans and Other Challenges to Comfortable Reality

Once upon a time . . .

There was a great kingdom that prided itself on being the smartest, the most logical, and the greatest at absolutely everything. And indeed, the kingdom was rich and powerful and received lots of grant money donated from everyone important. The philosopher-king who ruled this magical land noticed one day that every time he saw a swan, it had white feathers. After consulting with his Truth Committee, he found that every single member agreed: No one had ever seen a swan with anything except white feathers. Thus, a theory was born:

All swans are white.

This theory was duly recorded in the Annals of All Truth for the kingdom. Once thus inscribed, it was added to every textbook in the land, so that all children were thoroughly trained in the principle—one hesitates to say "dogma"—that all swans are white.

One day, a naughty little girl listened to her teacher state that all swans are white. The little girl thought about that, then she stuck her grubby little hand into the air.

"Teacher!"

"What is it, Brunhilda?"

"What if they're not? I mean, what if all swans aren't white?"

Horrified by such heresy, the teacher set little Brunhilda to writing "All swans are white for sure" a thousand times. Brunhilda did as required, muttering all the while, "I still don't believe it."

Fast-forward decades later. Brunhilda is now out in the wilderness where she hears a swan honking from a pond nearby. Sneaking up on the pond, she peeks through the bushes . . . and sees a black swan!

At that point, she knows that she has toppled orthodoxy.

The point of this story is that if you have a theory that all swans are white, it takes only one confirmed sighting of a black swan to realize that the theory is incorrect.

This is the state of science today. Current scientific orthodoxy holds the theory that psychic phenomena are "impossible." With this theory held as "truth," any claims to the contrary are ascribed to hoaxes, frauds, mistakes, delusions, or hallucinations.[1]

As with the theory that all swans must be white, if any single psychic skill is demonstrated proven, it topples scientific orthodoxy that all psychic phenomena are impossible.

This book is an attempt to topple that scientific orthodoxy.

Please note, Brunhilda did not have to demonstrate that all swans are black, or even that black swans are particularly common. To disprove the theory that all swans are white, she only needed to find a single black swan.

Like many people, and certainly like most people trained in the hard sciences, I, too, grew up believing that all swans are white, that psychics were all jokes, hoaxes, and charlatans—fun entertainment, but with nothing real about them. I studied physics—as hard a science as there is—and spent a career in computer science, focusing primarily on artificial intelligence and neural networks. Things don't get much more logical and down-to-earth than that.

The problem is, when I started experiencing odd, inexplicable effects, I had to choose from three alternatives. I could dismiss my experiences as self-delusion, trickery, or imagination; I could decide I had lost my mind and tipped over the edge into psychosis; or . . . just maybe . . . I could have found a Black Swan.

Since by most reports people seem to believe I'm a moderately normal, functioning adult, I do not believe I'm psychotic.[2] On top of that, my Black Swan hasn't been a single event, but a bevy of Black Swans. They've come one right after another. They've come in whole bevies, flocks, *herds* of Black Swans. Some have come with hard physical proof.

It's pretty difficult to throw away the amount of data that I've accumulated from personal experience. In fact, the experiences are so compelling that I've had to completely change my perspective about almost everything I thought I understood as orthodoxy.

With that said, I also recognize that my personal experiences are compelling and convincing to only one person—me. No one else can possibly trust these experiences as meaningful evidence, because they were not generated in formal scientific protocols or under rigorous scrutiny. In fact, the only person who knows exactly what happened and what didn't happen is me.

I'm like little Brunhilda. I've seen my Black Swans and I know that current orthodoxy is wrong. Unfortunately, I also know that just as Brunhilda's word about what she has seen in that pond isn't sufficient to convince the philosopher-king to change the Annals of All Truth, my personal experiences, no matter how ardently I protest their veracity, will convince no one else that my Black Swans exist. To accomplish that, I need harder proof. And that hard proof is what this book is about.

In the chapters that follow, I'll guide you through a handful of the Black Swans I've seen. I'll tell you why I personally believe in these Black Swans, mostly because I've personally experienced them. But, recognizing that you'll need more proof than my personal stories, I'll also show you that each one of these Black Swans is supported by an extensive array of scientific evidence. In other words, you don't have to believe my stories. While I hope you enjoy them, and that they enliven your journey, you don't have to believe a single word I tell you about what happened to me. Instead, I ask you to believe the many scientists who have spent years of their lives and risked their professional careers and reputations to investigate the possibility that not all swans are white.

Over the following chapters, I'm going to invite you to observe eight separate Black Swans. There are other Black Swans out there that I won't discuss, of course, and to some degree, the ones I've chosen to discuss are those that have most intruded on my life. I could have included several more topics, but only at the risk of making this book excessively long and unwieldy. But here's a sneak peek at the beautiful Black Swans you'll meet in these pages.

The First Black Swan is psychokinesis, more specifically spoon-bending. I start there because whenever I do a workshop, I nearly always make time for a spoon-bending exercise. People love doing it. (And, yes, in my workshops they don't watch me bend spoons. I pass out spoons and forks and have the participants do it themselves. It's way fun.) Furthermore, it's something people remember; it sets them up for a good time. And . . . well, you'll read all about it in the next chapter.

The Second Black Swan is remote viewing. This is the skill that the CIA and the military spent more than twenty years developing by supporting a group of "psychic spies." You may think you know all about that program, and you may think you know that it was "discredited." If you believe that, I think you may find yourself quite surprised by what the evidence really shows about the effectiveness of remote viewing.

The Third Black Swan is energy healing. This is a Black Swan that surprised the heck out of me when it impinged on my life. As you'll learn in the stories I share about this particular skill, though I had learned to respect several other psychic skills, when healing showed up in my life I was completely blown away. Happily, there's a substantial body of evidence that supports psychic healing and, interestingly, the ability of prayer to affect the outcome of health crises.

The Fourth Black Swan is telepathy, and, as a related skill, something I call "telempathy." The dividing line between these is subtle. I consider telepathy the ability to read another person's thoughts. Telempathy, a word I coined, is the ability to read another person's emotions. To me, telempathy is easier to believe in, but as it turns out, the scientific evidence is pretty clear that telepathy works, too.

The Fifth Black Swan is animal telepathy. This Black Swan is near and dear to my heart. Like many of you, I'm a pet owner. Or rather, I should say I am proud to be allowed to share my home with my cat. I grew up with dogs and love them dearly, too, but in recent years I have switched to cats as my companion animals.[3] I find animal communication with my cat is both very real and amazing when it happens. In this chapter, you'll learn that there are some surprising experiments that provide good evidence for the ability of animals to read our minds, at least some of the time. Don't believe me? Read the chapter.

The Sixth Black Swan is precognition. If you thought it was hard to believe in animals reading your mind, when it comes to looking into the future, you may decide that is even wilder.

But as it happens, there is solid scientific data that demonstrates that we absolutely do have proof that we can look into the future. (I don't use the word "proof" lightly, by the way.) You might be surprised by this chapter, but I hope you'll be open-minded enough to read it.

The Seventh Black Swan is survival after death. Yes, that's right. I'm going to address the question of whether any part of us survives after death. To put this in perspective, I used to be absolutely convinced that there was no chance that anything survived the death experience. As a good little scientific materialist, I was completely convinced that death meant the cessation of everything. No heaven, no hell, no ghosts, no nothing. Death merely meant you just . . . stopped. I tell you some part of what has changed my mind about this, and then I review the solid scientific evidence that demonstrates that some part of us—a spirit, a soul, something—survives death.

The Eighth Black Swan is reincarnation. Yes, that's what I said. Reincarnation. By that I mean exactly what you think I mean: the whole prospect of having more than one life. In this chapter we take a look at cases where children remember lives they've lived before, and we consider how credible these cases may be. This again is a topic that once would have surprised me. Fifteen years ago I would never have imagined myself writing anything in support of reincarnation—that was simply far too strange for me. As it turns out, however, when I measure the outrageousness of the concept today, it's . . . not so much.

After considering each of these eight Black Swans, I recap what we've learned in chapter 9. I summarize the evidence presented and offer my own generalizations for what they imply about how psychic phenomena operate. No, I don't present a theory that attempts to explain how they work—I leave that to the professional physicists and theoreticians like Ervin Laszlo and Amit Goswami, who are working on such theories. These and other very smart men and women will no doubt eventually succeed and lead us into a better understanding of how the universe really works.

In the chapters ahead I have had to winnow through the available evidence. There are dozens and dozens of papers in each of these subjects that, for lack of room, I have had to leave out. I tried to find interesting, solid research projects, and wherever possible, I looked for experiments that maybe haven't been publicized as much as others. A glance at the reading list will show you that there is far more research out there than I have discussed, or could discuss in less than a one-thousand-page tome. With occasional exceptions, I limited my list of papers to only those published in the past ten years or so.

Because most people don't have access to the libraries where most of these academic papers can be found, however, I have also included a Recommended Books list. These are books that are favorites on my personal bookshelf, and all of them should be available in regular bookstores or libraries. All are well written and good reading.

Finally, experience has proved to me that many people who read a book like this will want to explore their psychic abilities for themselves. (And, yes, you do have psychic skills, even if you've never experienced them so far. If I can do these things, so can you.) Thus, I've provided some interesting resources that you can follow up on if you like.

Most of all, though, I hope you find this book fun and entertaining as well as informative. Although I take the subject seriously, the last thing in the world I want to do is bore you into submission. Instead, I hope you'll be entertained, enlightened, and set free to go discover your very own Black Swans. Reading about other people's experiences won't convince you of anything.

So go out and find your own. They're out there, just waiting for you to discover them.

In the meantime, however, it's time for you to meet my First Black Swan.

CHAPTER 1

The First Black Swan: Psychokinesis

I have a bowl in my house that is filled with the remains of various pieces of cutlery that are not exactly usable. These are forks and spoons and an occasional knife that used to be good-quality stainless steel cutlery, but which now are just . . . strange. Every so often I give a workshop for people who want to learn how to access their psychic selves. The format varies some, depending on the time available. Yet, no matter how long the workshop—a day, a weekend, or a week—the one skill people always want me to teach them is spoon-bending.

To be honest, I'm not quite sure why spoon-bending is so popular. It's really a bit of a party trick rather than anything profound. But maybe it's just that a warped fork is tangible evidence that they have done something unusual. When you go home with a fork that is bent and twisted into strange shapes, you have absolute proof that you did something extraordinary.

Spoon-bending is definitely a skill that has fallen on hard times. It had been extremely popular in the 1970s as celebrated psychic Uri Geller rose to fame as a spoon-bender extraordinaire, until in 1973, he was caught cheating on national television, on the *Tonight Show*. He was declared a fraud. He was pilloried by all and virtually drummed out of the United States.

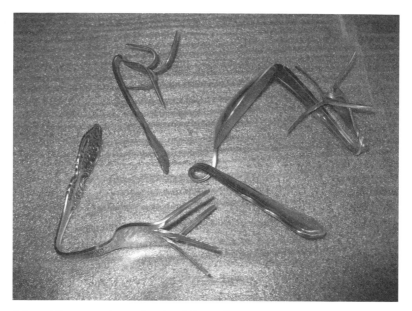

A few of the many pieces of cutlery left over from various workshops I've given in which I teach spoon-bending.

Now to be fair, Geller *did* cheat. Everyone agrees on that, even him. What is often not heard is *why* he cheated. According to his side of the story, he was blindsided by that request, not expecting to be forced into demonstrating his skills in that particular venue. Furthermore (again from his perspective) he was exhausted, stressed, and simply not in the right frame of mind to be doing anything psychic, yet he felt hounded to perform on television. Still young and desperate not to look bad by refusing, he resorted to cheating.

Do I believe this story? Well . . . perhaps. Knowing what I know about doing any psychic function, Geller's story is credible, at least in the basics. Psychic functions, like all other human talents, are not perfect all the time. No one—*no one*—can perform at their peak at any hour, day or night, or continuously, or on demand under stressful circumstances. That applies just as much to a top athlete, an exceptional musician, or a terrific student. Human beings simply aren't perfect. And the public pressure to be perfect—particularly in any psychic field where people are simply waiting for you to fail—is overwhelming. A young man (he was only twenty-seven at the time of that infamous *Tonight Show* debacle) who had grown accustomed to acclaim might easily be tempted to mix stage magic with psychic skills. So . . . I think the verdict is "unproven" in this case, no matter whether you're trying to prove Geller's abilities or his lack of them.

It is also true that after that episode, a number of scientific studies conducted in Europe under extremely rigorous conditions validated his innate ability to manipulate matter with his mind. Here in the United States, however, his reputation seems forever tainted by that Unfortunate Incident.

A decade ago, however, I would have laughed to scorn anyone who defended the "fraud" Geller. Why my change of heart? Because I can spoon-bend. And I've taught close to a thousand other people to do it, too. I now understand that not only is spoon-bending possible, but also most anyone can learn to do it—and pretty easily, too. I've taught people to do it in small workshops, and in huge ones with hundreds of people. And in one memorable interview on *Coast to Coast AM* with George Noory, he asked if I was willing to try to teach people to spoon-bend over the radio. I said I'd never tried that before, but I'd give it a shot. As it turned out, it was hugely successful, with one listener even calling in to say he had no cutlery handy, so he'd bent a large screwdriver instead!

A few years ago I was attending a workshop given by my good friend Robert Bruce. He is a renowned Australian mystic, whose work in energy and out-of-body experiences is some of the most effective in the world—and he's an incredibly charming and funny man in person. At any event, on the second or third day of this five-day program, I asked him if he ever used his energy exercises to teach people to spoon-bend. He told me he'd never done it himself, so he didn't teach it. Was I willing to show the group how to do that?

That night I went to the local KMart and bought enough good-quality cutlery for the smallish group to learn spoon-bending. When the time came the next day, I handed out forks (I strongly prefer to teach people using forks rather than spoons for reasons I'll explain later), and proceeded to use Robert's energy exercises to get people to bend their forks. As I have come to expect, everyone in the class succeeded brilliantly, and within fifteen or twenty minutes, we had a whole menagerie of twisted cutlery sculptures.[4]

The next morning, one of the women in the workshop came in and said she had to tell us what happened the night before. It turns out that this lady was dining with friends at quite a nice local restaurant. During the dinner, the talk turned to politics, a subject she was passionate about. She got a little, um, enthusiastic while talking with one of her friends. She was making her point rather forcefully and wagging her fork at the person she was speaking to, as you might wag your finger at someone. And . . . the fork drooped and melted in her hands.

She was *so* embarrassed!

She hurriedly pulled the fork out of sight onto her lap and, hiding her actions with the tablecloth, tried to put it back into its original form. She never did get it quite right, of course . . . the specific curves and angles of cutlery are difficult to replicate by hand, particularly under cover of a tablecloth when you're upset!

So the lesson from this is: If you must spoon-bend when you're dining out, spoon-bend *responsibly*.[5]

The bottom-line conclusion I have drawn about spoon-bending is that it is one of the absolute easiest psychic skills to learn, at least at the elementary level I teach it. (Far from television worthy, I might add!) And why do I prefer to teach people to bend forks rather than spoons? Because forks are a little bit harder. With a spoon, about the only thing a beginner can do is to twist the spoon at the neck, where the bowl meets the handle.[6] That's far too easy to do, even in fairly sturdy cutlery. But if you've ever taken a good-quality stainless steel fork and tried to bend just one tine with your fingertips, you know that it's all but impossible to do. I ask people to try to bend their forks with their fingers before we start the spoon-bending process, just to make sure they're convinced they can't do it. Only then do I start guiding them in how to spoon-bend.

The basic process is one of running energy through the fork to soften it. I teach people some simple exercises on manipulating chi energy; then I get them to run that energy through the fork for a few minutes, concentrating on setting their intentions that the fork soften and bend.[7] As they do that for a while—as little as a minute or two, or as much as five or six minutes, depending on how good they are at running energy and holding their concentration on what they're doing—the fork really does soften. At that point, they can bend, twist, warp, and distort it however they like—including twisting individual tines. When they have it twisted it into the configuration they like, they put the fork down and don't touch it for three or four minutes. When they pick it up after that break, the fork has "set" in that new shape and is as hard and stiff as it was before. If they want to change the shape again, they have to start the process from scratch.

It's true that my success rate is not quite 100 percent. I find that two kinds of people have trouble learning to spoon-bend.

One set is people who are themselves quite low in chi, or life energy. This is usually people who are elderly or who have a serious illness. They barely have enough chi to keep themselves going, let alone some left over for softening stainless steel.

The other type is someone who is convinced that it cannot work. Now, don't get me wrong. I've taught a lot of skeptics to spoon-bend, to their astonishment. The very first time I tried to teach spoon-bending, the group included a PhD physicist and a PhD anthropologist, each of whom individually assured me that spoon-bending was a total fake, all because of the flap over Uri Geller's *Tonight Show* debacle. Yet, they were willing to humor me and give it a try. They took less than five minutes to become amazing successes. The physicist in particular had ALS (amyotrophic lateral sclerosis), so he had very poor strength in his hands, yet he succeeded at bending his fork.

I also remember one workshop in which there was a participant who was a professional magician. At the break before we started the spoon-bending exercise, he came up to me and assured me that it was all a fake[8] and that he knew at least a dozen different ways to fake spoon-bending. I listened to him as he listed them all; then I assured him he wouldn't have to use any of those fakes in the workshop—he could do it for real. He was skeptical but had an open mind and was willing to give it a try. Twenty minutes later, he came up to me, showing a wildly twisted fork and jubilantly said, "I did it! I don't have to fake it anymore! I can really do it!"

The type of skeptical person who fails is the one who is so convinced that it can't be done that she refuses to actually try—or subconsciously refuses to allow herself to try. I ran into one of those in a workshop with a number of scientists. While claiming to have an open mind, when it came to the spoon-bending part, one in particular simply could not get her fork to bend. I tried everything I could think of to help her, short of bending it myself: running extra energy through it with her, helping her focus and concentrate, and so on. Nothing worked. I could see she appeared to be *trying* to bend it but . . . nothing. Finally, I actually touched her fork . . . and it was so soft it was practically like squishy butter! Clearly, she'd made it so soft and malleable that a small child should have been able to bend it—yet when I again encouraged her to try to bend it, she still claimed she couldn't, that it was too stiff. It seemed to me that her fingers were working against each other, something like doing an isometric exercise, where a lot of effort is expended yet nothing actually moves. My guess is that she has never been able to bend a spoon and likely never will.

As with any psychic (or physical) skill, you can convince yourself you are incapable of doing it. Yet, the truth is, as best I can tell from my totally unscientific observations of hundreds and hundreds of people, most people, possibly almost all people, can do spoon-bending. It's easy to learn, easy to do, and when you do it yourself—as opposed to watching someone do it on the stage—*you know for a fact that it's not a fake.*

And that's exactly why I teach this particular little party trick so often in workshops. When I teach people about chi energy, it all sounds airy-fairy and nonsensical to anyone with a scientific mindset—it certainly did to me when I first heard about it. Even when I show people that they can literally feel the energy moving around their bodies, they often have the same reaction I initially had, that it's all imagination and none of it is anything more than self-delusion. Yet, when I teach people to take that same "imaginary" energy, run it through a fork for a few minutes, and then feel solid stainless steel soften enough to become soft and malleable in their hands, suddenly what was nonsensical and imaginary becomes very, very real.

So perhaps that's the real reason for the popularity of spoon-bending. If you learn to do even one thing that conventional science deems wildly impossible, you begin to believe that other things are possible, too.

Spoon-bending is of course only one of many manifestations of psychokinesis. People have been known to have a wide variety of psychokinetic skills, including

- lighting light bulbs in their hands,
- sprouting seeds by holding them in the palm of the hand,
- moving objects without touching them,
- changing how dice roll or roulette wheels spin to force a specific result,[9] and
- influencing random events (such as with a random number generator) to force a specific trend in results over many, many trials.

Again, these are only examples of skills that have been studied. While my experience has been primarily spoon-bending, I did once try sprouting seeds in the palm of my hand. It was, well, not exactly either a success or a failure. Here's what happened.

I was preparing for a new workshop I planned, and I wondered if I could manage to teach people how to sprout seeds in their palms—in spite of the fact I'd never done it myself, nor even seen anyone else attempt to do it. Someone had mentioned to me that it was possible to do it, so I figured I'd give it a try. If I could manage the trick, I'd think about adding it to the workshop.

I got some vegetable seeds from my local nursery and gave them a little soak in water for about an hour. This particular type of seed was supposed to have a seven- to ten-day sprouting time once planted. After that brief soak, I sat down in my favorite meditation chair, put about three seeds in the palm of my hand, and started doing the same energy process that I use for spoon-bending. (I have no idea if this is how people who know how to sprout seeds do this—it's simply the process that I tried.) I was very careful to hold my hand steady by propping it on a pillow so I wouldn't accidentally tip it. I cupped my other hand over the one holding the seeds and started running energy between my palms. After a few moments, I felt something very odd—a flash of heat and light combined with a shock, a bit like an electric shock. Startled, I uncovered my palm holding the seeds to see if they had sprouted. They hadn't.

Instead, they'd disappeared.

So much for my seed-sprouting abilities. I never did add seed-sprouting to my workshops. Probably that's just as well, don't you think?

A couple of points about this aborted seed-sprouting effort are important. One thing is that when you're working with these energies, you sometimes get results that are not what you intend. Was I trying to make the seeds disappear? Not at all. It never occurred to me to even try to do that. Nonetheless, that's what I accomplished. Particularly in a case like this where I didn't have any idea what I was doing, never even having seen someone else do it, it was likely a little foolhardy on my part to attempt seed-sprouting. Maybe someday I'll get someone to show me how to do it correctly.

Another key point to remember is that the energies you work with when doing psychic work are significant. *These are not toys or games.* I cannot emphasize that enough. Working with life energy and altered states of consciousness is serious business. These energies are powerful and they can do things to you and to other people that are not so pleasant. Fooling around with psychic skills is highly risky unless you learn how to do it under the guidance of a competent, caring, and highly ethical instructor. It is especially risky when you lack the discipline and maturity to use these skills wisely instead of arrogantly. While not quite as dangerous as handing a four-year-old a loaded pistol to play with, the impact of careless, irresponsible "play" in these arenas can have serious consequences.

On second thought, maybe playing around irresponsibly with psychic skills is *more* dangerous than handing a four-year-old a loaded pistol.[10]

If psychokinesis is impossible, what are we to make of other reports by researchers in which some amazing effects are noted? For example, Dong Shen reports on a Chinese experiment in which solid matter (a piece of paper) apparently passed through other solid matter (a capped plastic canister)—and did so instantaneously—or at least so quickly that no one observing the scene saw it happen.[11]

Shen described a program in which Chinese volunteers are trained to see a "third eye" screen behind their foreheads by entering a trained state of "second consciousness." When in this state, they can visualize an object being other than where it is— and the object relocates to a new location. Here's how it works.

A capped black plastic canister, such as that holding 35 mm film, is used to hold a piece of paper. The paper, prepared in secret, has something written on it, unknown to everyone except the preparer. The preparer also folds it in a personally unique way and places it in the plastic canister where the cap seals the paper inside. An independent observer monitors the preparation of the paper and the canister but cannot see what is written on the paper.

In the experiment Shen witnessed, the main participant was a seventeen-year-old with only a middle-school education but who had received approximately six months of training in accessing this second consciousness state. Once the canister was ready, the participant sat in a chair one meter (a little over three feet) away from a table. The canister was placed on the table. The two researchers plus five observing guests sat also between one and three meters (between three and ten feet) away from the table. No words were spoken during the experiment.

For about forty minutes, the participant focused his attention on the plastic canister. Neither he nor anyone else moved from their chairs. No one was close enough to the container to reach it. Other than staring at the container and occasionally looking up at the ceiling, the participant did not move.

After forty minutes, the participant announced that the paper was no longer in the container. It instead had moved about six meters away (nearly twenty feet) to the far wall of the room. The participant also announced that what was written on it was "830," in blue ink.

An observer checked that location and retrieved the paper. The person who prepared the paper verified his own handwriting, the content of the message, and that the paper was still folded in the idiosyncratic way he had folded it at the beginning of the experiment.

There it was, just as the participant had announced: 8-3-0, in blue ink.

There are many curious features about this experiment. First, the participant had no demonstrable psychic skills until undergoing the Chinese training program. Thus, whatever skills he possessed at the time of the experiment were learned skills. Second, although there were at least seven witnesses, all watching attentively, no one saw the paper move out of the cylinder and across the room. Furthermore, the paper, even folded as it was, was far too small and light to be able to be thrown for that distance (nearly twenty feet).

Shen describes the subject's efforts:

> *During the experiment he concentrated on the black car-tridge container and got it deep in his consciousness while entering into the SCS [second consciousness state]. Then an image of the container appeared on the third-eye screen located in front of his forehead. He saw the image of the paper in the same way. At the very beginning, the paper image was not stable and not clear. After he focused on the image for a while, it became stable and clear on the screen. The number on the paper could then be easily read, that is 830 written in blue, even though the paper was folded inside the capped container. When the image of the paper was clear on the screen, he started to use his mind to move the paper out of the container. At a certain point he "saw" in his mind that the container was empty and saw in the room that the paper was on the floor near the wall.[12]*

It's easy to dismiss reports like this. They're clearly idiosyncratic to this subject. The researchers make no claims that everyone can achieve effects like this. And yet, cultural biases should not lead us to ignore reputable reports, even if they're not conducted in western European or American institutions. The Shen report discusses the prime candidates for training in psychic skills as being children between the ages of eight and twelve (prepubescent) or young adults between fifteen and twenty-two years who have limited education—in other words, people who don't know that they're doing something that isn't supposed to be possible.

Is it the case that we educate our children out of a whole range of abilities by informing them that they can't do them? Does the Western mindset force psychic phenomena underground?

What Is a Meta-Analysis?

Often, a single study doesn't generate convincing results, particularly when the size of the study is small. Generally, the most trusted form of evidence for or against an effect is not a single study but an analysis of *all* studies that have been done on that effect. Doing a meta-analysis is tricky, however, because studies are typically done by different researchers, using different protocols, with different degrees of care in study design.

The primary reasons researchers do meta-analyses are because they are more general than any one specific study. In addition, meta-studies can determine if any type of publication bias is occurring. They also tend to demonstrate if an effect is specific to one particular researcher or one specific study protocol or if it extends to multiple researchers and protocols. This process also increases the total number of participants or trials—and in statistics, more data means more significant data. If you flip a coin five times, it's not all that unusual to get five heads in a row—it happens about 3 percent of the time. But if you flip a coin fifty times, the odds of getting fifty consecutive heads (or fifty consecutive tails) are about 1 in 1 quadrillion (specifically, 1 chance out of 1,125,899,906,842,620). In other words, if you flipped fifty coins every second, it would take you well over *thirty-five million years* before you flipped fifty consecutive heads or fifty consecutive tails.

There are many ways that meta-analyses can go wrong. First, the analysis is only valid if it includes *all* studies published on a particular subject (or at least all studies in which necessary analysis information is included in the study report). How individual studies are encoded and selected for inclusion in a meta-analysis is a subjective process. A meta-analysis can be considered trustworthy only if it explicitly defines the criteria for selection and the methodology of encoding the studies in advance and explicates those criteria and methodologies in its report.

All this is well and good, but what is the scientific evidence that these are not just amusing and interesting anecdotes? Does science in any way support the reality of these experiences?

As it happens, it does.

Several types of psychokinetic effects have been put under rigorous scientific scrutiny. These typically are experiments in rolling dice to see if it is possible to influence the outcome or in attempting to influence random-number generators to output nonrandom-number sequences.

The short answer to this type of experiment is that across about fifty years of studies, the effect is small but highly statistically significant. For example, a 1989 meta-analysis of a half century of controlled dice-rolling experiments showed highly significant influence of participants on selecting the roll of a standard die. The results were so significant that the chance that they're merely statistical flukes is more than a billion to one.[13]

In 2006, a controversial meta-analysis of psychokinetic effects was published by Dr. Holger Bosch, Dr. Fiona Steinkamp, and Dr. Emil Boller, from various European organizations. This study, which for convenience I'll refer to as the BSB study, performed a meta-analysis of human interaction with random-number generators. It is one of the more frequently cited studies by skeptics as disproving psychokinesis.

Basically the BSB study searched hard to find a reason to discount the possibility of psychokinesis. While noting that there are strong statistical data supporting psychokinesis, and that this evidence is generally of quite high quality in terms of the methodology used to collect the data, the authors came down firmly on the negative side of the question of whether psychokinesis is real. They concluded,

> *the statistical significance of the overall database [of studies of human interaction with random-number generators]*

provides no directive as to whether the phenomenon is genuine ... Publication bias appears to be the easiest and most encompassing explanation for the primary findings of the meta-analysis.[14]

In part, their claim that publication bias was responsible for the supposed psychokinetic effects was as a result of their use of a funnel plot to identify such bias. (See "What Is a Funnel Plot?") The resulting chart clearly showed an asymmetric funnel, which is commonly interpreted as meaning that larger effects come from smaller-scale studies. When this happens, these small-scale studies are possibly statistical flukes, like tossing only five heads in a row instead of fifty heads in a row.

What Does Publication Bias Mean?

Not all research studies ever see the light of day in peer-reviewed journals. The reasons studies may never be published include two critical ones—and these reasons undermine how science should be conducted.

The first such problem is that a study in which the results are inconclusive, or oppose the researcher's expected results or (worst of all) pet theory of the world, very often are stuck into a file drawer somewhere and never written up. This is horrific for science since it generates a tremendous bias in favor of currently popular theories while suppressing data that tend to undermine those theories.

The second problem is that a study may be written up and submitted to appropriate journals, but those journals may decide that the study outcomes are either results they choose not to present (often because they undermine existing accepted theories or belief structures) or are simply "uninteresting" because they merely confirm existing theories. The problem with that is that having more data that supports a theory means that confidence in that theory is more secure.

What Is a Funnel Plot?

A funnel plot is used in meta-analyses to determine if publication bias exists in the reported studies. Basically, it plots the magnitude of the effect against the sample size in each study. Ideally, it might look something like the plot shown for a meta-analysis with each data point representing an individual study included in the meta-analysis. If the funnel plot is not symmetric, it implies that there is some type of publication bias, either for or against the effect as a result of the sizes of the studies. In other words, small-scale studies might show favorable results, while large-scale studies do not (or even might show negative results).

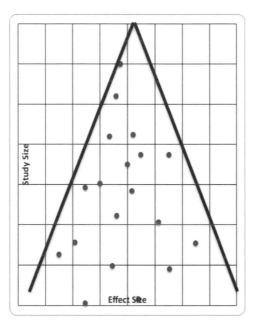

The dark lines on the chart reflect the 95 percent confidence level for the studies, that is, that there is 95 percent confidence that the studies' correct results are between those lines based on a statistical analysis of the studies and the data..

Continued

What Is a Funnel Plot? *(continued)*

Usually, the study size is represented by the statistical standard error of the measured effect. Most commonly, the study size is on the vertical axis, and the effect size is on the horizontal axis. This type of plot is convenient because a quick glance at the distribution of the studies can demonstrate whether they're approximately symmetrically located within that 95 percent triangle, as are the dots in the example diagram. If they are approximately symmetrical around the center line of the triangle—the vertical that runs through the peak of the triangle—there is no obvious publication bias; if they're not evenly distributed, if they lean more to one side or the other of the center of the triangle, it means there is a *possibility* of publication bias. Or there might be some other reason for such a distribution.

Problems can arise with using funnel charts, including the possibility that there really is a difference between large-scale and small-scale studies. Also, depending on how study size and effect size are defined, the shape of the chart can change quite dramatically.

The BSB study, as noted in the concluding statement quoted earlier, also ascribes the positive results shown by psychokinetic studies to the "file drawer" effect in which negative or inconclusive studies are simply buried in file drawers and never written up for publication. (See "What Does Publication Bias Mean?")

Doesn't look too good for psychokinesis being a genuine effect, does it? Well, not so fast. As it turns out, there are some serious issues with this highly publicized meta-analysis that show up only when the actual process used in the BSB study are examined in detail.

Dean Radin, Roger Nelson, York Dobyns, and Joop Houtkooper responded to this meta-analysis with an assessment of the quality of the BSB study itself.[15] They note a number of serious problems with how that study was done. One problem is that the BSB study was itself quite selective in how it chose to include or exclude previous research reports in its meta-analysis. One specific research report sort of included in the BSB study reported results from a total of seven individual experiments, yet only one of these was included in the BSB study analysis. Furthermore, the four largest studies included in the BSB report all had their data seriously underreported—and those four studies contained more than three hundred times as much data as all the other small-scale studies included in the BSB report combined. These four studies by themselves are so large that Radin et al. claim that "the overwhelming preponderance of data in these large experiments should be taken as definitive . . . [because] the remainder of the meta-analytic database [in the BSB study] comprises less than half a percent of the total available data."[16] In other words, the BSB report threw out the vast majority of the data available for its meta-analysis, giving excessive weight to the small-scale studies while ignoring the statistically more important large-scale studies. That's definitely *not* how a meta-analysis of anything should be conducted.

Radin et al. also noted that in addition to throwing away nearly all the relevant data, the BSB study also literally threw away two-thirds of the potential studies that could have been used in the meta-analysis. As noted in "What Is a Meta-Analysis," one of the huge mistakes made in a meta-analysis of anything is arbitrarily ignoring previous research papers and including only a selection of them—the selection that matches the bias of those doing the meta-analysis. *All* data and *all* previous research needs to be included to construct a competent meta-analysis, not just data or research that supports the biases of those doing the meta-analysis. This is not the case in the BSB study.

Radin et al. reported yet another key problem with the BSB study that is far too common in modern-day science. This error is called "experimenter's regress." Specifically, the BSB report concludes,

> *this unique experimental approach will gain scientific rec-*
> *ognition only when researchers know with certainty what*
> *an unbiased funnel plot (i.e., a funnel plot that includes*
> *all studies that have been undertaken) look like. If the*
> *time comes when the funnel indicates a systematic effect,*
> *a model to explain the effect will be more than crucial.*
> *Until that time, Girden's (1962b) verdict of "not proven".*
> *. . with respect to dice experiments also holds for human*
> *intentionality on RNGs [random number generators].*[17]

As Radin et al. note, specifying this kind of criteria is set-ting up a Catch-22 requirement for psychokinesis. Here's why. When an accepted theory predicts outcomes of an experi-ment, the theory is tested merely by comparing experimen-tal results with those theoretical predictions. If they match within the limits of experimental error, everyone rejoices and says the experimental protocol and measurement methodol-ogy was "obviously" correct. Unfortunately, if experimental data and accepted theory don't match, the presumption is that it must be the experimenter's fault. The design of the experi-ment or the protocol or the methodology must be wrong. Or the experimenter must have been perpetrating a fraud. Or the participants in the experiment must be hoaxing the experi-menter. Or something. It can't possibly be that the *theory* is wrong because, well, *simply everyone* believes the theory, right?

Right.

Certainly it's true that not all studies of psychic effects are well designed. Yet, at the same time, as the BSB study demonstrates equally clearly, many of the studies that "disprove" psychic effects are very poorly done and display a shocking amount of researcher bias, poor protocols, and other mistakes that invalidate the conclusions drawn by the skeptical authors. In other words, if it's important to demand scientific care in paranormal scientific reports—and it is—it is equally important to demand the same type of scientific care on those reports that attempt to debunk those studies.

Because no coherent theory exists for psychokinesis (or any other psychic phenomenon), and because mainstream thought—the "accepted theory" in today's science—is is that psychic phenomena simply don't exist, any experiment that demonstrates a statistically significant psychic effect *must be wrong*. In other words, rather than letting actual, measured, real-world data control the theory, theory overtakes observation. We're not allowed to measure the effect until we have a theory of how psychokinesis (or any other psychic phenomenon) works, but without data, it is impossible to construct a coherent theory of how it works.

Catch-22.

Before leaving this topic, I need to point out one other little detail that virtually proves our ability to impact physical matter solely with the mind. In the 1980s, Jack Houck became seriously interested in spoon-bending. As it happens, he had access to metallurgical analysis equipment. As reported by Paul Smith,[18] Houck investigated the crystalline structure of metal that had been psychically deformed (which Houck referred to as "warm forming" the metal to avoid sensationalizing his reports), compared to metal that had been mechanically deformed (as happens in all magician's tricks, such as when the spoon is surreptitiously pressed against the edge of a table, or previously deformed with a vise and a pair of pliers). He also compared those with the structure of metal that had been subjected to extreme heat (such as a torch). Houck took cross-sections of the three types of deformed metal and compared their microstructures to determine what types of cracks, if any, each type of deformed metal had at that microscopic level. Here's what he found:

Metal deformed mechanically, as a stage magician does it, showed cracks in the structure. Metal deformed by extreme heat showed a set of crystals that had been fused and melted. But metal deformed using "warm forming" (that is, the psychically bent spoons bent at ordinary room temperature, or at least skin temperature), however, showed neither the fused and melted crystals of being subject to high heat nor the cracks of mechanical deformation. Instead, *at a microscopic level*, they had an intact crystal structure, as if they had been manufactured in that physical shape. In other words, the psychically bent spoons had the same microscopic structure as if they were *melted and cast* in the deformed shape. As can be seen in the photos of some of the psychically bent cutlery from my workshops, such a set of silverware would be *very* interesting, if not too functional.

Examples of cutlery bent by participants in my workshops; the spoon is a tablespoon, not a teaspoon.

The melting point of stainless steel is approximately 2750° F (1510° C). I don't know about you, but my hands simply don't get that hot. (Ow!) While skeptics may claim that it's possible to fake spoon-bending (and it is, in lots of different ways), I know of no way to fake it that preserves the microscopic structure of the bent spoon or fork as found by this research.

What's even more interesting is that science has *known* for more than thirty years that psychokinesis works. Isn't it interesting that it is still dismissed as a party trick? All I can say to that is:

Some party trick, huh?

CHAPTER 2

The Second Black Swan: Remote Viewing

A few years ago, I got a call from a friend who lived in a town about half an hour away. He had a favor to ask. One of his friends, a divorced mother and a real estate agent, had disappeared with no warning. Her purse and house keys were found in an empty house she had listed, but her car also was missing. A search had been on for more than twenty-four hours with no sign of her. My friend gave me only her name, her time of disappearance, and that she'd left purse and keys behind in an unlocked house. As for me, I had never heard of this woman, much less met her or seen a picture of her. My friend asked if I could use my remote viewing skills to try to locate her.

Let me digress for just a moment to explain just a little about remote viewing. You might remember in the mid-1990s that the CIA talked about having funded a series of programs using "psychic spies" for more than twenty years. I'll have much more to say about that program later, but for now, the key point is that much of the money the CIA spent went toward remote viewers.

Remote viewing is a form of clairsentience ("distance sensing"), where the psychic perceives information that is far beyond his or her five physical senses. In the case of remote viewing, it refers to being able to see locations far away or hidden—even halfway around the world—and which the viewer has never visited. The protocols and procedures for remote viewing tend to be fairly strict, but the key one to understand now is that the remote viewer will do much better the *less* she knows about the targeted location.[19] The other point is that a viewer can focus in on anything—a place, a set of coordinates on a map, or a person.

I'm not the world's best remote viewer in large part because I don't practice it very often. As with all psychic skills, to be really good at it, you have to practice daily, just as a concert pianist has to practice every day. I don't have the time or the interest to do that practice, so I'm merely so-so as a remote viewer, which means that I'm not necessarily reliable. There are times I'm dead-on accurate and times I'm way off in what I sense.

Still, when my friend asked for help, and was so clearly worried about his friend, I couldn't say no. I agreed to do a remote-viewing session and report back to him on what I observed. It would be up to him to determine whether to report any of the information I got in my session to the police or the family.

Once I got off the phone, I took care of a few chores, gathered some materials, and settled into my favorite comfy chair to do the session. Because I'm merely a competent viewer, when I have an important session such as this, I play a recording of a take-home exercise from the remote-viewing training program I took a couple of years earlier. The hour-long recording provides audio support for a solid remote-viewing session and helps me focus and stay on target. I put the CD in my player, plugged in the big earphones, and settled down to relax. I had a clipboard, several sheets of blank white paper, and a few pens. At the top of the paper, I wrote my instructions for this session: "Describe the location where G. A. is now."

An hour later I had several pages of notes, sketches, and so on. The most important thing was that I had a strong sense that the woman was dead. I also had a sense of the location, the position of her body, what her hair looked like, and so on. I believed she was lying half curled on her side in a depressed area, like a ditch, with something vertical on either side of her. It felt to me as if she was outside, and that it was very near a place where lots of cars drove by. I even had a description of her. There were a lot more details, too. I dutifully wrote up my results in a long email and sent it to my friend.

Two or three days later, her body was found. Unfortunately, it was not where I had seen it, but in her car, which was parked in the parking garage of a regional airport sixty or seventy miles away. Apparently she had committed suicide.

When I got that news, I was disappointed in myself. It seemed to me I was completely wrong and my remote viewing session was a bust. The friend who requested the session sent me a picture of her from her obituary notice, and it looked nothing like the woman I had seen. The features were pretty close, but the hair was all wrong, in a long, curly cloud around her shoulders, whereas I had seen a woman with hair like a smooth, tight cap against her head—possibly either cut very short or longer hair tightly pulled back in a bun. That was yet another miss, I figured.

I called my friend Deb in Toronto to tell her that I had proved I was a pretty bad remote viewer. She had a somewhat different take on the session, however. She suggested that I take my notes and do some research to see whether I'd gotten any details right. Maybe I wasn't *completely* wrong, after all. Out of curiosity—and because I knew that sometimes I really could be amazingly accurate—I agreed to do that.

The first thing I did was pull out the four or five pages of notes I'd taken during my session and create a list of every single fact I had come up with in the session. I excluded nothing whatsoever. Anything I noted in the session went on that list. When I was done, I had a list of about fifty or sixty "facts."

The next thing I did was to go online and research the newspaper reports from her hometown paper to see what facts I could verify. To my astonishment, the first article I found online showed her in a completely different, more recent picture than the one my friend had sent me. It was a virtual duplicate of the image I'd gotten in my session! Her hair was pulled back tightly in a tight bun-like style.

More heartened, I scoured every article I could find to determine how accurate I had been. I ranked everything as either a "hit" or a "miss." Every item was assumed to be a "miss" unless I could find a specific published detail that confirmed exactly what I had said. If I could find no information about an item, that counted as a "miss." I went down my list of items and started assessing each item individually.

Between 70 and 75 percent of them were "hits."

Of the "misses," several items were in that category because I could not find any published information to confirm or refute them. If I were right about those additional items I could not confirm one way or another, I would have been between 85 and 90 percent accurate.

Of course, I got some things badly wrong. She was not lying in a ditch, for example. I marked everything I noted about her location as a complete "miss," but it's entirely possible that some of the details were right on the money, such as being half curled on her side in a depressed area like a ditch. It's hard to imagine how a person could be found dead in a car without being in a similar position, with seats and dash making a ditch-like appearance.

But when I reviewed the session notes, barring the incorrect information about *where* she was, nearly everything else in the session was correct.

If you have never tried remote viewing, this type of result seems almost astonishing. How could I possibly discover any information about a woman I'd never met or seen while sitting quietly in a comfortable chair in my own home, tens of miles away?

The very first time I ever tried to remote view, I was at a week-long seminar. The remote-viewing exercise in that seminar was very simple. About two dozen of us were in a large room sitting around tables. We were given plain white paper and pencils. The leaders for the workshop revealed a flip chart on which some latitude and longitude coordinates were printed. We were given no real direction except to "describe the target at this location."

Latitude and longitude are not my strong point. I had no clue what location they indicated, so I didn't try to figure it out. Instead the first thing I drew was a simple arc, very similar to the image here. I fiddled around with it a little bit, adding some more detail, running water and a sense of green behind it and so on. Then I thought to myself, what would it look like if I saw it from above? And again I sketched the arc, this time with something very round in front, more swaths of green, and water. The only thing I could think of was that the whole thing reminded me of the St. Louis Arch, although the shape seemed too narrow, and I had no idea what the round thing was.

After a few minutes, the trainers asked us to put down our pencils. After going around the room and asking everyone to talk about their impressions of the target, I was convinced I was completely off base. Several people had gotten a sense that the target was the Black Hills, so I figured I was off by several hundred miles. Other participants were all over the place. No one else pointed to a location anywhere near St. Louis. Once we'd all revealed our ideas, the trainers displayed two photographs of the target.

Not only was the target the St. Louis arch, but also the angle of the first photo showed it in a virtual exact match to the curve I had drawn. And the second photo? That showed the arch in the background, and the round Busch Stadium in the foreground, in the exact position of the peculiar round thing I had drawn. In fact, my two drawings were so accurate they were practically tracings of the two images of the arch.

To say that I was completely freaked out would be a mild understatement. This was one of my first experiences with doing anything that someone would call "psychic," and that exercise is what led me to take further training in remote-viewing.[20]

While I found my experiences remote viewing enlightening, I'm aware that they don't really convince anyone except myself, since only I know what "really happened" and whether or not my experience was in any way faked. (It wasn't, but again, my attestations don't count for anyone else!)

The real question is whether substantial data exists that is scientifically valid and that supports the idea that remote viewing works.

Remote viewing is one of the most commonly discussed, and perhaps most poorly understood, of the psychic phenomena. A lot of misinformation about remote viewing is out in the popular press and even among people who claim to be remote viewers and who use the term too loosely. As used specifically here, I use the term to refer to a process that follows constraints of specific *protocols* in which a person perceives information about a location that is physically remote and for which the person has no direct sensory (or telemetry) source of information. That's a pretty complex statement, so let me take a moment to break it down.

First, remote viewing isn't just thinking that you know what's happening at your mother-in-law's house in Poughkeepsie, New York, when you're in Burbank, California. The reasons this doesn't qualify include the following: You (presumably) know about your mother-in-law's house and her habits and personality, you may have information about what she might be or probably is doing at any specific time, or you may have other information about her personal schedule or have received that information at some time in the past even if you've consciously forgotten it. When you think about your mother-in-law, you also know exactly what your target location is—her house or her person. In addition, you (also presumably) have an emotional connection to the subject of the viewing—whether that connection is good or bad. Just as with a doctor treating a family member, the presence of a personal relationship (good or bad) can skew results in a remote-viewing experiment. Thus, if a relationship is present, it's even more important that the viewer be completely blind as to who is being viewed.

In other words, a situation like this is not a "blind" reading. In a blind remote-viewing session, the viewer does not know where the target is. Sometimes that means they don't know the *specifics* of the target in terms of a particular building or other location. Sometimes it means they don't even know in what part of the world it's located. In a fully blind experiment, the viewer doesn't even have a guide such as map coordinates and doesn't know if the target is a location, a person, or an object. The target could be *anything, anyone,* or *anywhere.*

Don't get me wrong. It's possible that some level of psychic skill is involved in knowing what your mother-in-law is doing from three thousand miles away. However, that does not qualify as a remote-viewing "hit." It may be telepathy or some other form of clairsentience. Or it may just be a good guess.

In remote viewing, the process follows a *protocol.* This means that there are specific guards against the viewer finding out the information in any way other than through nonlocal perception. What might such a protocol look like? Let me walk you through a typical training exercise in the remote-viewing program where I trained.[21] This will not be exactly like any of the exercises we did in that program, but it does illustrate the overall training process.

The students gather in a room and each is handed a different sealed manila envelope. The outside of the envelope has nothing but a numbered label on it, perhaps something like "Target 2." Inside that envelope is a photograph of a location anywhere in the world or an object. The student receives no information whatsoever about what is in that envelope other than that every target envelope is different.

Furthermore, the instructor who hands out the envelopes doesn't know what is in them either. The envelopes were prepared by someone not directly participating in the course in any way at all, not as instructor or assistant instructor or in any other role in the course. The envelope preparer is not present at the training course and never learns which envelope goes to which student viewer.

Once the students have their envelopes, they split off either individually or in pairs. If in pairs, one student acts as a "monitor" prompting the one acting as "viewer" with appropriate questions or asking for clarifications. The idea is for the monitor to keep the viewer on track and away from errors as the viewer attempts to sense the object or location pictured in his or her envelope. (Remember, the monitor has no clue what is in the viewer's envelope either!)

What Does the Monitor Do?

The monitor's job is to watch what the viewer says and notice when she starts using nouns as her perceptions. When the viewer starts *naming* things instead of *describing* things, she's probably in trouble. For example, if the viewer starts saying something like "I see an apple," it's highly likely that the next thing she'll report is some association with "apples" in her life experiences: apple pie, Mom's apple pie, Mom, Mom's house . . . aha! This is just like Mom's house.

That set of free associations is called "analytical overlay," or AOL in remote-viewing speak. And it's a bad thing because it nearly always means the viewer has stopped being focused on the target and instead is focused on his or her own memories.

Continued

What Does the Monitor Do? *(continued)*

Thus, when the monitor hears a noun, he will gently ask the viewer something like "what is it about the target that reminds you of an apple?" In this way, the viewer is nudged back into *describing* the target by saying something like "It's round and red." Now, that description just might mean there really is an apple at the target. On the other hand, it also might mean the viewer is looking at a round red leather ottoman or a large round barn or any of dozens of other round red things.

The other task of the monitor is to notice when the viewer is getting stuck and not getting new perceptions. At those times, the monitor suggests that the viewer move forward or backward ten feet (or any distance), or the monitor may ask what the target looks like when viewed from above or from behind. There are cases where a viewer initially reported that the target was just a blank white screenlike area. When the monitor suggested that the viewer turn around and look at what was "behind" him, the viewer then realized he was mentally standing with his nose practically pressed to a blank wall in a room with the target object behind him in the center of the room!

The students can do the actual remote viewing in any of several *methodologies* presented or by using their own techniques. (I'll have much more to say on methodologies later.) They are given perhaps twenty minutes or so, after which the students switch roles, with the monitor acting as viewer to view the image in his or her own envelope, and the viewer then becoming the monitor to guide that viewing session. If a student is conducting a viewing session alone, he must stay aware of when he slips into using nouns instead of adjectives and remind himself to consider the target from multiple perspectives (above, farther back, closer in, from behind, etc.).

When all the sessions are complete, one by one, the students meet with the instructor, with their notes and sketches of their session as viewer, along with their still-sealed envelope. After briefly reviewing those notes and confirming that the envelope has not been opened, the instructor takes out a corresponding envelope labeled "Judging 2." (Remember that all these envelopes were prepared by someone other than the instructor or any program participants, so the instructor has no idea what is inside any of these envelopes.) In the judging envelope are four photographs, labeled A, B, C, and D, one of which is the correct target, with the other three photographs being other objects or locations.

Together the instructor and the student assess the four pictures for points of similarity with the notes the student took. The student tries to determine which of these four images he or she viewed in the session. The instructor merely guides this process but does not control it. His role, similar to that of the monitor, is to ask questions and let the student answer them. In this process, three of the photographs are eliminated and a "winner" is selected. Suppose the chosen winner is photograph C, perhaps a photograph of a man riding a bicycle along a city street.

Once a winner is selected, the instructor opens the actual target envelope to see what the target image was. If the image is one of a man riding a bicycle along a city street, bells ring, fireworks go off, and the student gains a tinsel crown to wear. (I'm kidding. The instructor says, "Good work.") If the image is one of the other photos, the instructor and student try to figure out what went wrong by analyzing the notes of the session and the four judging photos.

It's important to note the key characteristics of this training protocol:

- The *viewer* has *no knowledge* of what the target is. None. Zero. Zip. Nada. This includes not knowing what *type* of target it is: a place, a location, a person, or an object.

- The *instructor* (the person assigning the task to the viewer) has *no knowledge* of what the target is. None. Zero. Zip. Nada.

- The *monitor* (the person guiding the remote viewing session, if there is someone in that role) has *no knowledge* of what the target is. None. Zero. Zip. Nada.

- The instructor doesn't even know what the *possible* targets are. Someone else, *never* present in the training program, determines the targets and the judging packets, codes them, and seals those envelopes before the instructor receives them.

- The instructor and the students have no information about the contents of the judging packets until after the session is complete and the judging packet is opened.

- No two students *ever* get the same targets or the same images in the judging packets. That includes students in different classes that may be held months or years apart. Every class and every student gets new sets of targets and judging packets that have never been used before.

- The numbered label on the outside of the envelopes is used solely to ensure that the judging packet for a given student includes the target for that student.

- The protocol does *not* specify what *methodology* the student uses to do the viewing. Any methodology that complies with the protocol standards is acceptable.

This protocol is far more challenging to establish and follow than you might imagine, particularly when you have a lot of students in a lot of classes. Notice that it is also a protocol that you *cannot* perform by yourself. Remote viewing, properly conducted, requires a *team* of people—an absolute minimum of two people, and preferably at least three: one to generate the target and prepare the target and judging envelopes (or website), one to assign the now-blind target, and one to do the viewing.[22]

You can get by with only two people under certain circumstances, such as my viewing the location of the missing woman. In this case, the person who assigned me the target was himself ignorant of where she was located. The feedback on whether I was correct came only after a third party (the police) located her body and reported on her location.

The idea behind all these rigid protocols is to eliminate any possibility that the viewer is not actually remote viewing but instead gathering information by (for example) reading the instructor's mind about the actual target image or by using prior factual knowledge about the target location, person, or object.

So what is the difference between a *protocol* and a *methodology*? The protocol, as explained above, is the set of restrictions on how the remote-viewing session is conducted, in terms of keeping target information away from the viewer or anyone connected with the viewer. Ideally, the viewer has no idea who determined the target image, for example, only that "someone" generated a target.

In contrast, the methodology is the process that the viewer uses to gather information about the target in the remote viewing session. There are tons of remote viewing methodologies, and some of them are fanatically rigid. For example, one protocol demands that the viewer have a specific brand of pencil, that the location of the remote-viewing session be set up in a specific configuration, with various objects in specific orientations to each other (pencil to the right, paper oriented just so, etc.). Other requirements specify how notes on the perceptions must be organized, the required use of ideographs (initial scribbles that help connect viewer to target), and so on. In the program where I learned remote viewing, we started with using audio signals to train our brains to go into specific remote-viewing altered states; later in the program, those signals were taken away so we could learn to access those states without the audio crutch.[23] All of those are valid ways of actually doing the remote-viewing session itself. No matter what methodology is used, however, the point is to give remote viewers a set of habits that they can fall back on to help them connect with their targets.

I was extraordinarily lucky to be taught by an instructor who understood this, and who provided us with information about many different methodologies, and who encouraged us to experiment with whichever ones seemed comfortable. Why do I say that? It's because there is one gigantic problem with protocols that require highly rigid methodologies. Those methodologies become a crutch. Suppose a viewer learns to view using only a specific brand of pencil or a particular "gray room" environment (i.e., a room in which everything is a neutral shade of gray or beige). If that viewer is ever called on to do a remote-viewing session when that pencil or that gray room is not available, the viewer often cannot do it. They have become dependent on the external aspects of the methodology instead of focusing on the internal state of accessing information about their targets.

With this understanding of what I mean by remote viewing, let's now consider the evidence of whether it's real.

It's now well-known that the military and the CIA and other intelligence agencies funded remote-viewing programs for more than two decades. Clearly, someone in the military or intelligence realms believed that something valuable was coming out of this program to maintain funding for so long. While the military is not known for being conservative in spending, it is also true that more than two decades of funding, across a half dozen presidencies from both parties, means that the agencies were gaining some level of satisfaction with the results of the program.

This is not the place to review the spectacular successes demonstrated by the best of the various military programs' remote viewers. Others, who actually participated in these programs, have already done that.[24] Instead, I'd like to consider the strength of the scientific studies that assessed the value of the results from those programs.

The government research program began in the 1970s based out of government contractor Stanford Research Institute (SRI), run by Harold Puthoff and Russell Targ. Later, after the reality of the remote viewers had been established to the satisfaction of the main funding agencies in Washington DC, the program moved to become more of an investigation of how remote viewing worked. In this process, operation of the program shifted to Science Applications International Corporation (SAIC), another large government contractor. In other words, the later experiments were not trying to demonstrate that remote viewing worked as much as they were trying to explore how it could be developed and used for practical purposes.

As you may recall, in the mid-1990s a report was commissioned to determine whether the remote-viewing program had been effective at developing valuable intelligence about meaning-ful targets (as opposed to training targets of no strategic value, for example).[25] You also may recall that this report was widely reported in the mass media as "debunking" the "wasteful" money spent on psychic research. However, if that's all you know about that report, you have an extremely misguided understanding of what actually happened.

First, all but one of the researchers selected to write that report were self-proclaimed "debunkers" of all things psychic *before they looked at the evidence.* In other words, far from hav-ing an open mind, they already had their minds made up before they started. The principal author of the study, Dr. Ray Hyman from the University of Oregon, has publicly stated on several occasions, both before and after this report, that he would *never* believe any evidence for the paranormal was anything except faked (or the result of poor scientific procedures) because any such evidence would violate his view of how the universe works. Hmmm . . . that does not sound very scientific, does it? What happened to the concept of letting the measurements and the data tell us the truth about the world?

I should note that there was one author of the study who strongly dissented with the hatchet job being done on the pro-gram. This was Dr. Jessica Utts, a highly respected statistician from the University of California at Davis. In a paper summa-rizing her conclusions about the SRI and SAIC, she listed nine significant points that the final report either omitted or glossed over:[26]

- Allowing the viewer to offer a free response (i.e., gener-ate an assessment in their own words) was "much more successful" than experiments where the viewer tried to choose from a list of a few possibilities (such as viewing one of a half dozen designs on a card).

- A few people were not just good, but extraordinarily good, generating highly repeatable results under a variety of protocols and conditions.

- About 1 percent of those who were tested were in this set of really good remote viewers. The similarity to the frequency of other human talents such as professional-level musical or athletic ability was striking.

- In this early study, training programs were fairly poor at improving the ability of remote viewers' consistency.[27]

- Feedback (i.e., telling the viewer the correct answer after the session ends) appeared to improve viewer morale, but it was unclear to what degree it improved actual performance.

- The distance between the target and the viewer was irrelevant. It was as easy (and accurate) to view a target halfway around the world as it was to view one next door.

- Electromagnetic shielding (i.e., putting the viewer in a copper-lined room to negate any electromagnetic signals) had no effect on the viewer—in fact, studies since then have given some slight indication that such a "Faraday cage" might improve accuracy by shielding the viewer from distractions.

- The evidence for *precognitive* remote viewing (i.e., viewing a target *in the future*) was, in Dr. Utts' word, "compelling." I'll have much more to say about this subject in a later chapter.

- There was no evidence in these experiments for psychokinetic interactions between the viewer and the target—in other words, the viewers did not or could not interact to affect the target physically.

Dr. Utts also found substantial evidence of support for these conclusions in research conducted in several other laboratories. In other words, the hallmark of scientific evidence, that experiments can be repeated with similar results by other researchers in other locations, was met handily. In fact, she concluded,

> the results . . . show that remote viewing has been conceptually replicated across a number of laboratories, by various experimenters and in different cultures. This is a robust effect that, were it not in such an unusual domain, would no longer be questioned by science as a real phenomenon. It is unlikely that methodological problems could account for the remarkable consistency of results shown.[28] [my emphasis]

Furthermore, let me quote from another paper written by Dr. Hyman, in which he explains his conclusions about the investigation:

> I agree with Jessica Utts that the effect sizes [i.e., the results of the experiments] reported in the SAIC experiments and in the recent ganzfeld studies probably cannot be dismissed as due to chance. Nor do they appear to be accounted for by multiple testing, file drawer distortions, inappropriate statistical testing or other misuse of statistical inference . . . So, I accept Professor Utts' assertion that the statistical results of the SAIC and other parapsychological experiments "are far beyond what is expected by chance."

> The SAIC experiments are well designed and the investigators have taken pains to eliminate the known weaknesses in previous parapsychological research. In addition, I cannot provide suitable candidates for what flaws, if any,

might be present. Just the same, it is impossible in princi-
ple to say that any particular experiment or experimental
series is completely free from possible flaw.[29]

In essence, what Dr. Hyman is saying here is that yes, the evidence is extremely strong statistically, far beyond any event caused by chance. Yes, the experiments (in this case, those done by SAIC) were well designed. No, he cannot suggest any flaws in the design. Nonetheless, the experiments *must* be flawed because, well, just because. They must be flawed because Dr. Hyman cannot accept that they might, in fact, be accurate representations of how the universe works—and because such a universe does not fit in Dr. Hyman's mental model of how the universe *should* work.

If you have followed with me this far, you should now recognize that the supposed exposé of the government remote-viewing programs was both less than objective and less than convincing. Only researchers who have an open mind, convinced of *neither* side—neither a true believer, nor a die-hard debunker—can objectively view the evidence. Dr. Utts was such an observer—but her commentary on the programs was suppressed, distorted, and even omitted from the final report. The problem with Dr. Hyman's perspective (and those of other such debunkers) is that when a truly objective view is taken, the evidence is quite astonishing. Dr. Utts' clear-eyed, objective survey of the evidence collected across more than twenty years of government research demonstrates not only that remote viewing can be done, but also that most people can do it to some degree or another.

The one disagreement I would make with Dr. Utts' list of nine conclusions is that it is now possible to train people to remote view. With an excellent training program, nearly everyone can learn how to remote view with reasonable success. Heck, if I can do it, anyone can—and as noted earlier, I can do it, sometimes quite well.

More than that, some very talented, hard-working people can do it extraordinarily well, with extraordinary accuracy, and extraordinary repeatability.

CHAPTER 3

The Third Black Swan: Energy Healing

About four years ago, I had a problem. While I can remember no particular incident that sparked this damage, I unexpectedly found myself with a very sore knee. Over the course of several weeks, my right knee became more and more sensitive. It swelled up to at least twice its normal size. It was red and radiated heat you could feel from several inches away, a clear sign of inflammation. I could not straighten it fully, nor bend it fully, without severe pain; for any comfort I had to keep it at a half-bent position and not place any weight on it. Truthfully, it reminded me of the severe rheumatoid arthritic knees my grandmother had suffered, though I'd never heard of rheumatoid arthritis popping up out of nowhere over the course of two or three weeks. I canceled a couple of activities because I didn't think I could stand for more than a few minutes at a time.

Nothing I tried made any real difference. I was popping aspirin regularly and trying hot and cold compresses, to no real purpose. The pain was so bad that sometimes it woke me up at night. I was in misery.

One day, I was whining on the phone about my knee to my friend Deb, who lives in Canada, about 750 miles away. After chiding me for not telling her sooner, she offered to do some energy work on my knee to see if it would help. With a "can't hurt/might help" attitude, I let her do her thing over the phone. I was pretty skeptical about energy healing, particularly when there was obvious physical damage such as was clearly the case with my knee.

An hour later, I was just flat-out flabbergasted. *While we were on the phone*, the pain in my knee stopped. It just . . . stopped. It had been with me twenty-four hours a day for about three weeks, and suddenly, the pain was gone. While talking with Deb, I found I could straighten my leg fully with no problem. I could bend it fully, too, again with no problem. I could stand up and had no problem with it bearing weight. The redness and heat radiating from my knee had also completely stopped. While the swelling dropped a lot on the phone, it took another couple of weeks before it also completely disappeared.

But for all intents and purposes, in that single hour on the phone, my knee went from getting-worse-daily to all-but-cured.

In the years since then, my knee has been 100 percent pain-free. No problems. Whatever Deb did, it was a *permanent cure* to whatever ailed my knee.

To be truthful, I hadn't paid a lot of attention to the power of psychic healing until this incident. I've never felt myself to be much of a healer, and though I incorporate healing exercises in the workshops I do, it's simply not a skill I practice a lot. If anything, I mostly work with animal healing rather than people healing.

I didn't quite know what to think about this experience. It was something I mentally gnawed on for quite a while, trying to decide what I thought about it. Then, it happened again.

The spring after what I now refer to as the Mysterious Knee Incident, I decided to do some work on my yard. For anyone who knows me, this is akin to an agoraphobic deciding to go to a rock concert. I really, *really* hate yard work. A lot. But my yard— which is far too big in my opinion—has this really long fence around it, and it's hard to mow close to that fence. So one clear calm day, I got a big jug of extended-release heavy-duty weed killer and decided to spray around the fence line in my yard, so weeds and grass wouldn't make for a messy fence. The weed killer was the type that came with a long wand that sprayed the liquid exactly where you wanted it. I was very careful with this potent poison, though just as I was finishing up about an hour later, a breeze did kick up a little bit.

When I'd put away my materials in the garage, I immediately took a hot shower, changed clothes, and immediately washed my yard clothes in hot, soapy water to get rid of any residue that might have sprayed on me.

A couple of hours later, I sat down to write in my journal . . . and that's when I realized I had a serious problem. I had no control over my right hand. And by that I mean *no* control. Not only could I physically not grasp a pen, but also I could no longer move my thumb to touch my palm below my little finger. Even if I managed an awkward a grip on a pen, I had no fine motor control in my right arm or hand whatsoever. I could barely scribble, so I could forget about writing anything legible. Also, there was a major palsied tremor in my hand, especially in my thumb. To make a bad situation worse, I seemed to be losing more and more control over my right hand and arm as the minutes ticked by.

My immediate guess was that somehow, in spite of all my care, I had accidentally absorbed some of that extended weed killer through my skin. I had poisoned myself.

This time, instead of waiting, I immediately called Deb, explained what had happened, and asked her to do her energy-healing thing. I think even she was skeptical she could do anything about chemical poisoning, but she gave it a try. This session was shorter, about forty minutes or so. But at the end of that time, my hand and thumb, instead of getting steadily worse as they had been before I picked up the phone, were back to normal. Once again, whatever Deb did was a *permanent cure* because I've never had a problem with my hand or thumb since.

Both these experiences have left me with a serious question: How am I to make sense of incidents like this?

Energy healing—the type of healing that my friend Deb practices—has a long, fabled history. It's also the type of healing Western science most often ignores. Despite that brush-off, more and more highly reputable medical researchers are investigating the role of energetic medicine and its efficacy. If you doubt that, take a look at the Reading List at the back of this book—I included only a sampling of papers and articles published in the past five or ten years, most published in reputable, peer-reviewed journals. It's worthwhile to take a look at some of these studies to understand what researchers have discovered about energy healing. I was fairly selective in choosing papers to include, but I could have included several times as many. An enormous amount of research on energy healing has been done in the past ten years or so.

Let's take a detailed look at a couple of studies of how energy healing can help specific diseases.

Dr. Adina Goldman Shore published a study in 2004 in which she studied the long-term effect of energy healing—specifically Reiki (see "What Is Reiki?")—on forty-five adult patients who reported either having depression or being under strong stress.[30] Ages of the participants in the study ranged from nineteen to seventy-eight. Dr. Shore did not include those who were diagnosed with severe depression or physical illness (such as stage IV cancers), or who were taking medications that had psychotropic properties (antidepressants, amphetamines, tranquilizers, etc.). Some patients did have diagnosed conditions beyond depression, however, including multiple sclerosis (MS), borderline personality disorder, chronic fatigue syndrome, nonterminal cancer, fibromyalgia, and similar conditions.

What Is Reiki?

Reiki (pronounced *ray-key*) derives from Buddhist practice. Various styles of Reiki have been developed by several Masters/Teachers over the past ninety years or so. The idea is that a Reiki practitioner can transmit healing energy or qi (also called chi) to a person in need of healing. There are three levels, or degrees, of Reiki practitioners: First, Second, and Master/Teacher. First Degree practitioners can heal themselves and others; Second Degree practitioners can heal at a distance; and Master practitioners can teach others how to do Reiki. Although there are several styles of Reiki, developed by different Master/Teachers, "hands-on" Reiki typically does not require actual touching of the client, but rather running hands directly above the client's body, a few inches away. Clients are typically clothed throughout the procedure.

Dr. Shore divided the participants into three groups. Thirteen of the forty-five received hands-on (nontouching) Reiki treatments; sixteen received distance Reiki; and sixteen received distance Reiki placebo. For those receiving distance Reiki, the practitioner and the participant were as much as several hundred miles apart during the scheduled times of the treatments. Obviously, those receiving hands-on Reiki knew they were getting some kind of treatment, so to ensure that this did not skew the results, the participants were all told that only some would receive actual Reiki treatments, whether distance or hands-on. The other participants would receive either mock distance Reiki or mock hands-on Reiki. Thus, even those who had a practitioner in the room with them apparently giving them a treatment could not be sure if it was a real Reiki treatment or a mock treatment. (In fact, of course, all hands-on treatments were genuine Reiki.)

The Reiki practitioners consisted of a dozen Reiki Masters, who were attuned to the most sophisticated level of Reiki, and three Second Degree Reiki practitioners who were specifically known to be capable at both distance Reiki and hands-on Reiki. To test the abilities of the practitioners, Dr. Shore received treatments from each and confirmed that she could feel the movement of energy through her body and experienced a sense of healing and relaxation from those treatments. Each practitioner also had to meet qualifications in terms of years of experience performing Reiki and number of clients treated.

In this study, the practitioners gave the participants sixty- to ninety-minute treatments—whether distance healing, hands-on healing, or placebo treatments—in a comfortable, quiet room once a week for six weeks. The treatment protocol was established prior to the study and followed a strict sequence: front of the body at the top of the head; down the body at specific points—eyes, temples, throat, heart, upper belly, midbelly; back of the body, starting with the back of the head and moving to the shoulders, neck, back of the heart, and the lower back; and finally ending with sealing in the energy and smoothing the energy field of the participants. The focus of these treatments was defined as healing the participants rather than meeting any study goals.

In accordance with standard research practice in medical studies, Dr. Shore used well-respected measurement instruments that have been used in a lot of psychological studies over the years. These were three key surveys, the Beck Depression

Inventory (BDI), the Beck Hopelessness Scale (BHS) and the Perceived Stress Scale (PSS). All three of these surveys have been validated for internal reliability (i.e., questions that basically ask the same thing in different ways will generate similar responses), validity (i.e., the survey measures what it's supposed to measure because its results correlate with independent diagnoses or measures), and test-retest validity (i.e., giving the survey again at a slightly later date to the same group gives very similar results). These characteristics are, to a great degree, the gold standard of testing in the social sciences, including psychology. In other words, they're excellent instruments with which to measure a person's perceived depression, sense of hopelessness, and stress.

So what happened? Here's where it gets interesting. At the start of the study, the three groups (hands-on Reiki, distance Reiki, and placebo distance Reiki) demonstrated no significant differences in their measures of depression, hopelessness, and stress. Yet, after six weeks of sessions, the two groups who received Reiki showed significant reductions in their perceived stress, depression, and hopelessness. The group that received no treatment (other than lying quietly in a calm room for an hour or so each week) showed slight decreases in perceived stress and depression but a significant *increase* in hopelessness.

Even more interesting, in a one-year follow-up with the participants, the significant improvements in those receiving Reiki were maintained! Dr. Shore expected that over that length of time the participants would gradually return to their prestudy levels of stress, hopelessness, and depression. In fact, that did not happen. Instead, there was a continued decrease in stress and depression, while the hopelessness increased very slightly but was still significantly below prestudy levels. The group that received no Reiki continued to have significantly worse results on all three measures than the two Reiki groups.

There's another interesting aspect of this study. Comparing the hands-on Reiki with the distance Reiki revealed absolutely no significant difference in effectiveness. Furthermore, even those in the hands-on group who believed they were receiving no actual Reiki treatments continued to experience long-term improvements in their emotional state for a year after the study, despite receiving no further treatments. To make this even more telling, those in the nontreatment group who believed they were receiving actual Reiki experienced no improvement in their scores, either after six weeks or at the one-year follow-up.

As we consider this study, first it should be noted that this was carefully crafted and took pains to be scientifically valid. The measurement tools used were ones widely accepted in social science and psychology as valid tools for measuring depression, stress, and hopelessness. The participants did not know whether they received Reiki treatments or not. Even those who received hands-on treatments were told that it might be a fake treatment, leaving them uncertain (other than by results of the treatment) whether they received it or not. Those who did not receive a treatment still spent an equivalent time each week lying in the same type of environment as those who did receive treatments. That placebo treatment had the potential to relieve stress simply by forcing sixty to ninety minutes of quiet relaxation each week.

Furthermore, consider how the study protocol was set up. The investigator who conducted the study understood the energy process she was studying, in this case, Reiki. She created a study that was designed to enable the Reiki practitioners to provide treatments in a supportive environment, rather than under glaring lights of a laboratory. Because Reiki, like all energy-healing techniques, is strongly dependent on the skill and ability of the practitioner, it is essential that studies of Reiki take into consideration the conditions under which Reiki can succeed. Dr. Shore also ensured that the practitioners were expert in Reiki before using them in the study.

Shore's study has answered one question about my experience with Deb's healing: For a skilled practitioner, it doesn't matter if the patient is under her hands or hundreds of miles away. Distance doesn't matter. Thus, the fact that I was more than seven hundred miles away from Deb at the times she healed me seems to be consistent with the results of this study. And that by itself is an astonishing realization. Distance does not matter in energy healing? The doctor can be hundreds—thousands!—of miles from the patient? No physical connection between the doctor and patient? Nothing?

Of course, Reiki isn't the only type of energetic healing by any means—it certainly isn't what my friend Deb used on me; she's not a Reiki practitioner.

There are dozens of studies and investigations in the medical literature on the effectiveness of energy healing, and the results are traditionally reported as "mixed" or, when the reporter is sufficiently skeptical, as presenting "no scientific data to support using energy-healing techniques." Such conclusions directly contradict not only my personal experience as I have described it above but also the results of carefully crafted studies such as Dr. Shore's on Reiki. Why is that?

Perhaps it is because the study Shore produced is an anomaly and other studies don't reflect that success. Consider a "study of studies," called a meta-analysis, of the use of various therapeutic touch energy healing on patients with cancer. Such a study was done in 2008 by a collection of undergraduate nursing students under the direction of Melody Eaton, PhD, MBA, RN, at James Madison University.[31] The students perused the literature to find papers that reported on the effectiveness of therapeutic touch (in any form) on patients with cancer. These students did not limit the collection to a particular type of therapeutic touch nor in how the studies were carried out. All papers included in this meta-analysis involved using some type of therapeutic touch healing on patients with cancer.

How Is a Meta-Analysis Conducted?

One of the ways researchers evaluate what has been done before is by doing a "study of previous studies." In essence, they first collect papers that report research results on a particular problem, in this case, studies that tried to use therapeutic touch healing on cancer patients. They then evaluate each study according to the "quality of the evidence" in seven categories as shown in the table below (adapted from Jackson et al., 2008):

Level	Description
I	A systematic review of randomized, controlled studies or evidence-based practice guidelines based on such systematic reviews (i.e., a meta-analysis)
II	Evidence from at least one well-designed randomized controlled trial
III	Evidence from nonrandomized well-designed trials
IV	Evidence from well-designed case studies with controls
V	Evidence from systematic reviews of qualitative and descriptive trials (i.e., no numerical measurements).
VI	Evidence from a single study or a qualitative (no numerical measurement) trial
VII	Evidence from authoritative opinions or "expert" reports

Studies in levels I, II, or III are considered more reliable than those in other levels. Each paper collected is evaluated and assigned a level. Then those studies are individually assessed, usually statistically using complex evaluations and comparisons, and a conclusion is drawn on the strength of the evidence that supports (or negates) the presumption of the study. The goal of a meta-analysis is to produce a study that is itself at level I.

Eaton's meta-study considered a total of twelve studies, three of them at level VI (i.e., a qualitative study with no numerical measurement) and the rest from well-designed, controlled studies at level II, III, or IV. Even though the papers used a wide variety of therapeutic touch systems, Eaton concluded that there was clear evidence that therapeutic touch relieved pain and anxiety in cancer patients. Despite mixing in multiple types of therapy (healing touch, therapeutic touch, Reiki, and other complementary types of energy therapy), the importance of the energy medicine to cancer patients was clear, leaving Dr. Eaton to recommend that nurses be trained in such therapies to better address pain in patients in a nonpharmacological way.

So, it works for cancer. Does it work for orthopedic issues, like my knee? Is there evidence to support using energy work on people who have bone fractures, osteoarthritis, fibromyalgia, or other joint and bone problems? In 2005, Ellen DiNucci published a comprehensive review of studies where energy healing was used in various orthopedic conditions.[32] Each of the studies was quite small, typically with fewer than twenty-five patients. Still, DiNucci found published studies that support the effectiveness of some type of energy healing for conditions such as the following:

- A small controlled study of twenty-five osteoarthritis patients saw significant reductions in pain and improvement in overall function of their affected limbs after energy healing using therapeutic touch.

- A fascinating controlled study in which bone cells from orthopedic patients placed in a growth medium which were in the intervention group received a type of therapeutic touch treatment. The treated cells saw significantly increased growth in osteoblast proliferation. This process is necessary to heal broken bones, so the implied result would be that patients with broken bones would heal faster if they receive therapeutic touch.

- A controlled study of fibromyalgia patients who received six weeks of either therapeutic touch therapy or a placebo version. The treated group had significantly lessened pain and improvement in functionality.

- An individual case study of a patient with phantom limb pain and peripheral neuropathy (damaged nerves) resulting from alcoholism and diabetes, who, over the course of several months, learned how to self-administer healing energy to reduce his pain from preintervention levels of 8 to 10 (on a scale of 0 to 10) to virtually 0.

- Another case report of a man with a broken elbow who received three treatments of energy healing over three days, after which his pain was reduced significantly, his anxiety reduced, and his ability to do regular daily activities improved.

These studies, as reported by DiNucci, may be small-scale, but they do make a strong case for continuing to investigate the application of energetic healing. And that is happening.

People have believed in nonmedical healing for millennia. No matter how lacking in religious zeal, all it takes for us to revert to our religious roots is to have someone we love in the hospital seriously ill. With very few exceptions, we revert to prayer to assist our loved ones to heal.

Until recently, such prayerful efforts have been scorned by science as mere superstition. Attempts to study the effect of prayer on hospital patients of various sorts have generated very mixed results. Much of the problem resides in the protocols used by scientists who study prayer's effect on healing.

Typically, such studies use prayer groups who do not know the person receiving the prayers. Often the prayer groups are scattered all over the country and know only the recipients' names and cities. Furthermore, in an effort to be nonsectarian, the praying groups often are from many different traditions, including religions that the recipient of the prayer does not acknowledge. Furthermore, scientists attempt to constrain the *method* of the prayer—something that in itself interferes in the process of producing meaningful prayer. Even if the studies generate positive results, they're criticized because they cannot control for family members who almost certainly are also praying for their loved ones. It becomes impossible to identify who is really being prayed for and by whom. Do prayers from loved ones have more efficacy than prayers from strangers? There is no way to sort that out given current study protocols.

Yet scientists are very clever people, and some have come up with a way to overcome these difficulties. Instead of having people pray for people who are ill, they develop a protocol in which people pray for nonhuman entities. This practically ensures that the only prayers being offered for the subjects are those mandated by the study group. Let me review one particular study of this sort to determine what the evidence from it shows.

Karen Lesniak was a psychologist at Jackson State University when she decided to study whether prayer could have an impact on healing in animals. She chose to work with bush babies, a kind of African nocturnal primate, which have a reputation for self-inflicted injuries when in captivity. There were twenty-two of these adorable little animals in her study group from the Jackson State University Center for Prosimian Studies. These particular animals tend to injure themselves during grooming because they spend too much time grooming specific areas of their bodies—a bit like constantly picking at themselves, which eventually opened up wounds.

The animals were assessed both by the size and severity of their wounds and by general laboratory tests for blood values. In addition, the animals were videotaped during grooming to record how often the site of the wound was groomed and the total amount of time spent grooming. The twenty-two animals were split into two randomized groups matched for similarities in physical condition; one group would be prayed for; the other would not.

The prayer intercessors were a Christian prayer group who regularly prayed for the healing of others. They were given the names of the animals and the desired outcomes to pray for, including an improvement in the efficacy of the medications used on the wounds and a reduction of the animals' stress and thus self-harming grooming behaviors. In addition, they were asked to pray that the wounds would heal. The groups prayed for the animals daily for four weeks, the length of the study, starting on the first day the bush babies received treatment. The condition of the animals was tested at the beginning of the study, at two weeks, and at four weeks, the end of the study.

So what happened?

Across virtually every measure, there were significant improvements in the group receiving the prayers compared to the group that did not. The prayed-for group showed increases in red blood cells, hemoglobin, and hematocrit levels. Even more important, the prayed-for animals showed significant decrease in the time spent grooming the wound and in the total amount of time spent grooming. The changes in behavior in the prayed-for animals were consistent with improvements in grooming behaviors. While cortisol reductions (a stress hormone) in the prayed-for animals were highly provocative, the small size of the study meant that this specific measure was not statistically significant. Yet the measured results clearly indicated a reduction in stress in the prayed-for animals. Stress resulted in the overgrooming that caused the opening of wounds, so any reduction in the animals' stress levels should improve their long-term outcome.

Many of the criticisms of human prayer studies do not pertain to this small but well-crafted study. There is no question that the control group (the group not being prayed for) did not receive prayers from outside the study. The measures of the outcomes in terms of the healing of the wounds and improvements in behavior—even the reduction in stress hormones—are objective measures of improvements in the prayed-for group.

The bottom line of this study is that the animals receiving the prayer showed significantly improved wound healing and an improvement in their stress levels and grooming behaviors. Prayer, at least in this study, somehow appears to make a big difference in the recipients.

At a minimum, if you know someone—whether human or animal—who is hurt in any way, pray for them if you can do so consistent with your beliefs. It cannot possibly hurt, and scientific evidence shows that there's a good chance it may help.

Another area where healing energy therapies have been studied is in cardiovascular diseases. Specifically, Barb MacIntyre, Jane Hamilton, Theresa Fricke, Wenjun Ma, Susan Mehle, and Matt Michel studied the impact of energy healing in coronary artery bypass surgery.[33] These investigators, all from HealthEast in St. Paul, Minnesota, at the time the study was done, considered the impact of energy healing on 237 elective coronary artery bypass patients, testing for length of stay in the hospital postoperatively, incidence of postoperative atrial fibrillation, use of antiemetic medications (medications to stop vomiting), the need for narcotic pain medications, functional status, and anxiety.

As with Dr. Shore's study, patients were randomly assigned into one of three groups: those who received Healing Touch treatments postoperatively, those who received visitors who did nothing, and those who received neither visitors nor Healing Touch therapies. There was no difference in the general standard of care administered to the patients by the hospital staff.

In this study, the Healing Touch group received three treatments, one the day before surgery, one immediately prior to surgery, and one the day after surgery. All the energy healing was done by two nurses trained in healing-energy techniques, and the patient had the same therapy provider for all three treatments. Compared to the Shore study, the treatments were considerably shorter, with the first and last being between twenty and sixty minutes, and only the one the day of surgery lasting as long as sixty to ninety minutes. Furthermore, treatments were done in a hospital setting, rather than in a relaxing healing room setting.

The control group received nothing except standard hospital care and attention from the nursing and medical staff.

The visitor group received visits of similar duration from a retired registered nurse the day before, the day of, and the day after surgery. However, this visitor did nothing except hold a general conversation with the patient while the visitor sat quietly in the room. Prestudy training ensured that the trend of the conversations was standardized across patients.

You might wonder why the visitor group was needed. Some have insisted that energy healing results from simply giving the patient extra attention on a personal basis rather than as a result of any energetic reason. By providing such extra attention in the form of the visitors, the researchers can discover if such an assumption was valid.

The results of this study are quite intriguing. No statistically significant difference was found in some of the medical measures, including the amount of pain medication needed, the use of antiemetic medications, and the incidence of postoperative atrial fibrillation—though each of those demonstrated nonstatistically significant improvements in those patients who received energy healing. On the other hand, those receiving the energy therapy experienced significantly less anxiety and had significantly shorter hospital stays than either of the other two groups.

As should be evident by now, there are a lot of studies that demonstrate the effectiveness of energy healing in improving patient outcomes for a wide variety of conditions, physical and psychological. If you want more, check out the reading list and select a few of the papers to review. You might be surprised by what you find there.

The point I'm making is that there are a substantial number of peer-reviewed, highly competent studies that demonstrate that energy healing directly affects the recipient both physically and psychologically. More than that, the healer does not have to actually touch the patient—doesn't even have to be in the same time zone as the patient. *Distance doesn't matter.*

All this is very confusing to those who are wedded to the contemporary notion of physical reality. We have action not only happening at a distance but also without any measurable connection between healer and patient. How is that possible?

Still, if you believe the scientific data, you must accept that *something* happens when capable energy healers do their thing. The question is, what exactly is it that they're doing? That remains an important—and so far unanswered—research question. There are some key factors that need to be attended to for those planning energetic healing studies:

- Energy healers vary in their abilities. Some are average, some are very good, and some are exceptional. Studies that use healers without first verifying their credentials may not generate the clear-cut results desired. Taking a weekend course in healing does not a healer make. The care used by Dr. Shore in verifying the abilities of the Reiki practitioners used in her study is part of the reason her results were so amazing.

- Energy healers vary in their techniques. I've mentioned a few techniques already, Therapeutic Touch, Healing Touch, Reiki, and so on, but there are many others. Some extremely talented healers, like my friend Deb, have their own individual style that doesn't correspond to any of the "standard" therapies.

- Energy healing best takes place away from a hospital setting. Hospitals are noisy, busy, stressful, and rarely calming places to be. Short of being in a quiet, private room, any energy therapy done in a hospital room is likely to be constrained by the environment. In the case of the MacIntyre et al. study, one of the healing sessions was delivered in an operating room—and there are few locations that would be more hostile to energy healing than that!

- Energy healers have quite different explanations about how they do whatever they do. Some talk about "transmitting" energy from themselves to the patient. Some talk about "channeling" energy from some outside Source to the patient. Some talk about not actually "healing" anyone but instead about simply helping the patient heal themselves. (My friend Deb is one of these; she refuses to accept credit for any of her healing successes.) The fact is no one really knows how they do what they do.

- It's possible that it isn't energy at all, but rather intentionality that is at the heart of energy healing. (Thus, it perhaps should be called intentionality healing.) Some healers, equally as good as the energy manipulators, claim that all they do is set their intentions that the patient be healed.

- Energy healing has to be done when the healer (at least) is in a special mental or psychological state. It corresponds to an altered state of consciousness, just as most of the other Black Swans discussed here do.

In spite of not really knowing how energy healing works, if you take the trouble to read some of the research papers on energy healing, you'll find that most of them present "theories" that explain the energy healing as if "that's the way it is." It reminds me a lot of the science documentaries on cable channels like Discovery or the Science Channel. They present theories such as, for example, that the dinosaurs were killed by an asteroid impact sixty-five million years ago. The theory is presented with great authority and as firm statement of fact. The scientific evidence is brought out and presented as conclusive proof that the theory is correct. Viewers watch those shows and go away believing that they understand how dinosaurs met their ends, until . . . a new theory is proposed that claims that dinosaurs were already dead when that asteroid struck, dead from disease or climate change or ingrown toenails. That new theory is presented as totally factual, until . . . The cycle goes on and on, with each accepted theory presented as "Truth" but none of them actually being true.

Human beings don't like uncertainty. It makes us feel enormously insecure and (maybe) a little dumb. We tend to cling to our beliefs as if they are Truth and fight tooth and nail to keep them in place. It takes overwhelming proof to convince many people that cherished beliefs about how the world works are wrong and need to be changed. In the case of energy healing, there are two key problems: (1) there exists no real theory, or at least no scientific theory, about how it works, and (2) there currently exists no real way to measure the energy (or intentionality) that somehow does the healing.

This leads us to a sticky problem. How do you convince the scientific establishment that energy healing works?

Luckily, energy healing is possibly the most accepted of all the Black Swans discussed in this book. It's not exactly mainstream science—yet—but some very mainstream organizations are investigating energy healing seriously. Organizations such as Scripps Center for Integrative Medicine, Harvard University, McGill University, Boston University, Los Angeles Orthopaedic Hospital, University of Iowa, Kaiser Foundation Hospitals, and many others have completed or are conducting ongoing studies in various aspects of medicine that don't fit into the current Western disease model of healing. Therapies as varied as acupuncture, body therapy, aromatherapy, healing touch, guided imagery, qigong therapy, massage, and Tibetan traditional medicine are just a few of the many therapies that have undergone or are currently undergoing study by esteemed academic institutions. Clearly some very smart people think there's enough in the concept of energy healing to justify doing some solid science to investigate it.

Before closing this discussion of healing—and it's one that could extend for the course of an entire book instead of a single chapter—I want to revisit the concept of intentionality.

What Is Intentionality?

Intentionality is related to, but not the same as, the concept of intention. Yet it differs from intention in some important ways. Intentionality implies that focused consciousness and awareness are directed toward a specific object or person. Intentionality implies that there is a purpose or specific effect directed at that object or person. Thus, intentionality brings to bear the entire aspect of the person expressing it, including consciousness, belief, will, and unconscious. Intentionality works in conjunction with consciousness to connect to underlying possibilities to bring about a desired outcome. In healing, it is used to manifest not a healing *energy* but a healing *consciousness* in the patient (adapted from Watson, 2002).

Rothlyn Zahourek, PhD, APRN, BC, HNC, describes intentionality in healers as comprising five key factors:

1. A desire in the healer for an outcome

2. A belief in the healer that the healer's actions will lead to that outcome

3. A desire in the healer to perform those actions

4. A skill in the healer to perform those actions

5. An awareness in the healer to fulfill the intention while performing those actions[34]

Notice that in this perspective, what matters is not what is in the patient, but what is in the healer. Given that the healer can only control herself, this is a sensible perspective.

One clear description of how intentionality can be used in healing is presented in a 2002 paper by Jean Watson, PhD, RN, HNC, FAAN, distinguished professor of nursing at the University of Colorado Health Sciences Center.[35] Her paper describes a theory of how intentionality works in healers. She points out that assisting in the healing process implies several key steps. These include the following:

- Healing the healer: The healer has to settle his own internal relationships with self and with other people.

- Discovering meaning: The healer has to discover compassion and meaning for the healing journey.

- Transforming suffering: The healer has to understand, embrace, and transform suffering, in himself and others.

- Understanding the cycle of life: The healer has to have a holistic understanding that life includes embracing both light and dark, birth and death.

Healing from an intentionality perspective isn't necessarily about finding a physical cure. Healing means doing what is best for the patient in accordance with those principles. It means assisting the patient in walking the same journey the healer has undergone, to guide the patient as she heals herself and discovers meaning in life, to transform suffering, and to understand the cycle of life. Once that is complete, whatever the physical state of the patient, the healing is complete.

With that said, however, it is also true that physical suffering can be so distracting and intrusive that other aspects of the healing journey cannot be taken until the physical suffering is reduced or eliminated. This is why so much of energetic healing may involve relief from suffering. Also, once that suffering loses its ability to use up the patient's energy, the body has much more energy available to heal itself.

Jean Watson provides a road map on how to achieve that form of intentionality healing, and it is worthwhile to contemplate her suggestions. If studied carefully, the path described can be seen in all healing traditions, whether energy-based or not. All healing traditions achieve their best results when the following steps are followed (adapted from Watson, 2002):

- Begin your day with a spiritual practice of some kind. Any that appeals to you will do, from qigong exercise to a few moments of silent prayer. Complete your practice by setting your intentions that you will have a good day, be present in the moment throughout the day, and set your intentions about all aspects of your day that you can control—but let go of things you have no control over. The goal of this is to encourage an attitude of caring compassion for all.

- Set your appreciation for healing as a spiritual practice, based in the soul. Trust that a universal Spirit, God, or the Divine are with you throughout your day, even when you do not sense its presence.

- Learn to be discerning in all you say and do. Keep your focus on the moment, and learn to bless and forgive everyone around you.

- Learn to see others more deeply. Other people do not always behave as we would wish—sometimes they are downright obnoxious. Work hard to look past the external appearance and behaviors to see the spark of divine that is within them.

- Embrace everything, the good and bad, as lessons that teach you to be more human and more divinely inspired.

- Set your intentions to meet these steps every day to the extent you can. Forgive yourself when you stumble—and forgive others when they stumble, too.

- Express your gratitude in the evening for the events of the day and the blessings and lessons the day has brought you.

- Cultivate your intentionality to be a true healer.

Being a healer is not necessarily an easy thing to do. It involves getting your own problems out of the way and focusing energy (or intentionality) on attaining the greatest good for someone else. Yet what is most interesting about this is not that it is challenging, but that it is possible. The scientific evidence of energy healing is clear. It exists. We may not have a clue how it works . . . but this Black Swan is alive and well.

CHAPTER 4

The Fourth Black Swan: Telepathy

A few years ago a friend of mine was going through a terrible time. His father was in the hospital and it was believed he was dying. A priest visited the hospital to administer the Last Rites since the doctors had warned he had only hours or days to live. Although his father was elderly, my friend, whom I'll call Steve, was deeply upset. It wasn't so much that his dad was dying—over the past months, the elderly man had developed many health problems and no longer could do most of the activities he loved so much. Steve's dad had lived a long life and a good one. But Steve knew that his whole life was going to be uprooted once his dad died. Steve spent his days in emotional turmoil, desperately unhappy over the imminent loss of his father and just as desperately worried about how that would change everything about his own life.

I knew for a fact how upset Steve was, even though he lived some thirty or forty miles away from me and was someone I met socially only every week or two. How did I know that? It was because for about two weeks, every minute of every day that Steve wasn't actively involved in doing something that engaged his attention, such as working at the family firm or talking with friends, he was mentally screaming in agony, and I was picking up those screams at my house. Those screams were so agonized that I would wake up in the middle of the night hearing Steve scream in my head. They would turn on and off abruptly in the daytime, but at night, they were nearly continuous for hours at a time.

I knew whose screams they were. I knew what caused those screams. I simply couldn't think of anything to do to ease Steve's pain. Platitudes that everything would be all right couldn't begin to ease the pain he was going through. In fact, I couldn't even really talk with Steve about it because I knew that he had no idea he was broadcasting his personal agony so loudly, and he probably didn't want anyone to know how much he was suffering. I did mention it to a mutual friend, who agreed that telling him about it when he was already in such pain would only worsen Steve's situation. He was trying hard to "be strong" for his mother and sister, and to have someone else recognize his pain would have embarrassed him deeply.

So, for two weeks, I suffered right along with Steve. It was a relief when his dad—to the surprise of everyone—was released from the hospital and sent home. It didn't last long, of course. Steve's father died three or four months later, but in the meantime, Steve had come to terms with his dad's imminent passing and was not nearly so agonized about it as he had been a few months earlier.

Then came the funeral.

I lost my own dad when I was in college, and my mother's death about fifteen years ago affected me deeply, so I fully understood the pain of losing your parents. Still, I had only met Steve's dad once or maybe twice, I knew that his physical condition before he died was terrible as well as extremely uncomfortable, and I knew he had lived a very long, full life. I attended the funeral as a show of support for Steve rather than because I felt any particular personal grief over his father's passing. I'd gone to the viewing at the funeral home a few days before with no problem, and I anticipated no difficulty attending the funeral.

That just goes to show what I knew.

The morning of the funeral, I drove to the church where the service was going to be held. I arrived early, before hardly anyone else had arrived, mostly because I'd never been to that church and I wasn't sure how long it would take me to get there. I was just fine . . . until I turned into the church parking lot. Suddenly, I was completely overwhelmed by waves of grief and suffering—not *my* grief and suffering, but those of everyone who was about to arrive to mourn Steve's father. I literally had to force myself to open my car door and step out. It felt as if I was being battered by wave after wave of emotional trauma. I had to totally focus on standing upright and walking slowly into the church.

I knew what was wrong, but I still wanted to support Steve, so I literally tottered into the church sanctuary. Thinking (somewhat foolishly) that if I sat far away from where everyone else was sitting it would be less painful, I took a seat in a pew in the far back corner and tried to meditate and build up a few defenses against this unexpected emotional battering.

It didn't work. Throughout the service I was constantly struggling simply to sit upright and to build some defenses against the emotions hitting me from all sides. When the service was finally over, I let virtually everyone leave before even attempting to walk out to my car. Though I spoke very briefly to a couple of friends who were still lingering outside the church, I knew there was no way I could attend the graveside service or the wake after that. I drove home, thankful to be away from the emotional trauma of everyone else's grief.

These events happened right in the middle of a period of about a year when I was struggling with what I called an excess of telempathy. "Telempathy" is a term I coined to describe a state where I remotely sense, not other people's thoughts, but other people's emotional states. For a period of a year or more, I spent a lot of time overwhelmed by other people's emotional angst, with no clear way to control or block those incoming emotional states.

Unfortunately for me, I wasn't picking up people's happiness. Nope, what I was sensing were people in trouble, usually my friends and acquaintances, from wherever they were in the world. In those circumstances, I generally knew whose emotions I was picking up, and I recognized that the emotions weren't my own emotional responses, even when I didn't know why that person was unhappy or in pain. I also didn't particularly have control over whose emotions I detected. Even now I can only suppose it's just based on who is in the most trouble, but I really don't know why I pick up emotions from some people sometimes, but not from others, or not from the same people at other times.

Telempathy obviously isn't all beer and skittles. In fact, in my experience it's mostly pretty darned uncomfortable. I worked hard for a number of months trying to figure out how to stop the flow of emotional suffering that battered me repeatedly over those months. Most of the time I didn't have any particular warning when the emotional waves overwhelmed me. By the time I realized what was happening, it was too late for me to erect barriers.

One way you can visualize what I was trying to do is to think of trying to shut a door. If there is a water leak on the far side of the door and you're trying to push the door closed against the flow of water, it's not too bad—as long as there's only a trickle of water coming through the doorway. But if the water is more like a raging flood, you can push against that door all you like, and you probably won't be able to close it. What was happening to me was akin to the flow of emotional information going from zero (or a trickle) to a raging flood in the space of a heartbeat. By the time I consciously figured out what was happening, it was way too late. I couldn't close that door and block off the flood of emotions no matter what I tried.

As I mentioned, I struggled to control this telempathy thing for about a year. I talked with my friends and tried every suggestion anyone could come up with, but nothing worked particularly well. I even visited another noted and highly experienced psychic several hours' drive from me, but her only response was "Why are you coming to me? I can't help you. You're stronger than I am."

Wonderful. Not especially helpful, mind, but wonderful.

Telempathy has other aspects, too. For a while, I was so attached to a couple of my friends that I would tell them that when they stubbed their toes, I would say ouch. Given that one of those lived about forty miles away and the other lived twenty-five hundred miles away, that was pretty amazing to me.[36]

Eventually, I did manage to get the telempathy thing under control, mostly anyway. But the degree of vulnerability that it imposed on my life was shocking. It was very challenging and not something I want to repeat any time soon. Yet even now, it's not completely turned off. I still get antsy when a friend is in trouble, and I still call them with no warning, only to find that, yes, indeed, they are deeply upset about something or hurting badly.

I might also note that sometimes the connection turns into an echoing of physical pain they're experiencing. If feeling someone else's emotional anguish is uncomfortable, feeling their pain—literally!—is even more so. Telempathy simply is not a psychic skill I can recommend to others. It's too darned painful!

Telempathy isn't the same as telepathy, of course. In telempathy, you receive a strong sense of someone else's emotional state. In telepathy, you know what that other person is *thinking*. There's a vast difference between the two. Yet most of the time, what gets tested in laboratories is telepathy, not telempathy, perhaps because emotional state is so difficult to measure.

So how do they test telepathy? The groundbreaking experiments in telepathy were done in the 1930s by Joseph Banks Rhine at Duke University. He concocted a special set of twenty-five cards, called Zener cards, with five copies of each of five designs. These were simple designs that were very distinct: a set of wavy lines, a circle, a star, a square, and a cross. The idea was that a carefully shuffled deck of cards would be given to a participant in the study, the "sender." That person was physically isolated from the other participant, the "receiver." The idea was that the sender would randomly draw a card and concentrate on the design of the card. The receiver would try to tune in telepathically to determine what design the sender was looking at. Since there were five different designs, random chance would expect the receiver to guess right about 20 percent of the time, one time in five. If the receiver correctly guessed the card significantly more often than 20 percent of the time, Rhine believed that meant some type of extrasensory perception was going on—and that it probably was telepathy.

Experiments with Zener cards have been done for nearly eighty years, but they are fraught with problems. One big problem is that the experiment is really, really boring to participate in. Don't believe that? Okay, take a set of ordinary playing cards and shuffle them. Ask a friend to be the "sender" and you be the "receiver." Send your buddy into another room, or do something to ensure that you can't see the cards. As your friend draws a card at random and concentrates on the card, try to determine just the suit of the card your friend is looking at, whether it's a heart, a club, a spade, or a diamond. When you get all the way through the deck, shuffle the cards, and do it again. In fact, go all the way through the deck 10 times, for a total of 520 cards. If your guesses are random chance, you should get about 130 of your guesses correct. If you get significantly more (or significantly fewer) of them correct, maybe you're psychic!

Go ahead and try this. I'll be waiting right here when you finish. (Can you hear the theme song for *Jeopardy!*'s Final Jeopardy! round playing? *Doo-doo-doo-doo, doo-doo-doo* . . .)

All done? Okay, now I'm going to prove to you how psychic *I* am. Before you tell me your results, I'm going to make a prediction. I'm going to predict that you didn't get through the deck ten times. No, wait, I'm going to predict you didn't get through it three times. In fact, I don't think you made it all the way through the deck even once. Why do I say that? Is it because I'm an incredibly talented psychic? Alas, no, at least not in this case.

I don't think you made it through the deck even a single time because this kind of experiment is just so incredibly boring. It's also really hard to concentrate on a meaningless card for extended periods, which makes it not only boring, but tiring, too. Imagine what it must be like to have to spend hours at a time guessing simple designs on Zener cards. Could anything be duller than that? If you had to do that experiment, wouldn't you be dying to throw a ringer or two into the list? "Wavy lines. Circle. Square. Wavy lines. Mona Lisa. Cross. Square." Or is that just me?

Rhine's original experiments were filled with procedural problems, and his experimental protocols did improve over time. Over the years researchers have learned to refine how to do experiments in ways that remove possibilities of either accidental or deliberate cheating. Nonetheless, researchers still make huge mistakes by subjecting their participants to boring protocols that wouldn't keep a lab rat happy. Boring isn't good for accessing psychic states. At the very least, researchers need to provide a treat at the end of a successful run. Go have a piece of candy as a reward.

Having addressed some of the problems with telepathy experiments, it's time to take a look at the evidence to support its existence. We've all read anecdotal stories about people who know that their children, or siblings, or parents, or twins are hurt, or people who experience the same pain as a loved one at the exact time that loved one is injured hundreds of miles away. Do well-controlled scientific studies support these anecdotes?

As it happens, yes, they do. Rupert Sheldrake is an iconoclastic and enormously creative researcher in Britain. If ever a researcher thinks outside the box, it is he. His 2009 study, with coresearcher Leonidas Avraamides, shows how modern technology can be used to study telepathic effects.[37]

This study decided to test whether people know who sends an email before they receive the email. This is a slightly more modern riff on people who know who's calling them before they pick up the phone.[38] Just as with telephone calls, it's not uncommon for someone to think of a person and—*boom!* An email from that person arrives in their inbox.[39]

In this pilot study, designed to test the feasibility of the experimental protocol, volunteers signed up on a special website. They entered their own names, plus the email addresses of three of their friends—their "contacts"—who had also agreed to participate. All four, participant and the three contacts, received a welcome message explaining the protocol. After a randomized delay of less than five minutes, one of the three contacts was randomly chosen to receive a system-generated email. This message said: "This is the telepathy test. Please send an email reply that will be forwarded to [the participant]. Do not attempt to contact [the participant] directly. Thank you."

The contact person wrote a reply message to the participant and sent it to the system. Once the system received that reply, the computer automatically sent a second message to the participant that said: "Dear [participant]: One of your contacts has sent you a message. Please reply and guess who has sent it. Thank you."

The participant then replied with his or her guess about who sent the message in question. Only after this message was received and recorded did the system forward the contact person's message to the participant. Each participant and his or her contacts went through this process for either six or nine times after random delays of up to five minutes between trials, with the contact sending the email chosen at random each time.

Note that this is an entirely automated process. The computer chose the contact to send the email. The computer determined how long the pause between trials would last. Because this was done via email, the times the emails were sent, the times the guesses were made, and the times the emails were delivered were all documented down to the nearest second.

When the data was collected, there were 175 correct guesses out of 419 trials, for a success rate of 41 percent, significantly greater than the chance expectation of 33 percent correct. (Because of the three possible contacts who might have sent the email, chance would dictate that random guesses would be correct one time in three, or about 33 percent.) The odds of this effect being from chance alone is one in ten thousand.

Sheldrake and Avraamides had speculated that this test would have a lower correct-guess rate the greater the time between when the emails were sent and when they were received by the participants; this time delay could be up to half an hour due to a variety of factors, including simple delays in the email system, contacts delaying typing in and sending messages, and so on. Thus, as part of the analysis, they considered the success rates for messages where participants made their guesses in three time periods: less than three minutes after the messages were sent, three to ten minutes after they were sent, and more than ten minutes after they were sent.

The success rate for the three periods is shown in the table below.

Time period between sending message and receiving it	Number of trials in this time period (% of total of 419 trials)	Successful trials for this time period (% of trials successful in this time period)	Odds of chance result for this time period
< 3 minutes	161 (38%)	68 of 161 (42.2%)	1 in 100
3 to 10 minutes	78 (19%)	25 of 78 (32.1%)	Chance result
> 10 minutes	180 (43%)	82 of 180 (45.6%)	3 in 10,000
ALL TRIALS	419	175 of 419 (41.8%)	1 in 10,000

What's interesting about these results is that the longer delays between when the contact person was concentrating on the participant (i.e., in the process of typing a message to the participant) and when the participants made their guesses had a somewhat better success rate than shorter delays. Sheldrake and Avraamides note that this is not a statistically significant variation, but there is that deadly "middle of the test" period in which the success rate fell to chance levels.[40]

No matter how you look at this data, it's clear that something interesting is happening about four times out of ten.

Lest you think this is an exceptional case, Dean Radin's meta-analysis of results of telepathy experiments through 1997 and going back to the 19th century noted that in experiments with a chance result of one in four, or 25 percent, the overall success rate was one in *three*, or 33 percent. The odds of this type of success of that many trials being due solely to chance are one in a million billion.[41]

There are a lot of ways to interpret my "telempathic" skills mentioned earlier. I think the best interpretation, however, isn't to get too picky about the label, but instead to focus more on the functional outcome of the information. Let me explain what I mean.

Several years ago I participated in a "ganzfeld" experiment conducted by academics. In this experiment, a friend of mine, whom I'll call Stewart, sat in a room in front of a television monitor. Meanwhile, I was sequestered in a separate room, where I was installed in a comfortable recliner. The researcher taped halved ping-pong balls over my eyes (icky!), and the room was gently dimmed. In addition, I had headphones over my ears, and I was left to relax while the experimenter went to her control room.

Once the experiment began, the computer selected a short video clip from a large library of choices and displayed the clip on the screen Stewart was watching. His job was to concentrate on "sending" that image to me as I relaxed in my little recliner cocoon. Meanwhile, I was directed to concentrate on trying to read the images from my friend's mind—to use my "telepathy" to discern details from the video clip he was viewing.

I've detailed the specifics of this experiment elsewhere, including reasons why it was a not particularly well designed experimental protocol.[42] But for my purposes here, the point is that this type of ganzfeld experiment is a common way researchers attempt to demonstrate (or debunk) telepathy. The assumption in a ganzfeld experiment is that the person watching the video, in this case Stewart, "sends" the details of the video to me as the "receiver." Thus, if I successfully get the details of the video, it must mean that I read Stewart's mind, right?

If you've been reading this book carefully, I'll bet you may have already figured out one of the problems with this experiment. As it happens, I totally nailed describing the video. I got the colors, the shapes, a sense of what happened in it, the setting, all the relevant details. In fact, my description of the video was dead on target. But my contention is that all those successful details had very little to do with telepathy. So if I didn't read Stewart's mind, how did I get all those details correct? (No, I didn't cheat.)

The fact is, I didn't accomplish that feat using telepathy in any form. The night before we were scheduled to do the experiment, I sat down and did a remote-viewing session with the target being "the video Stewart will be watching tomorrow afternoon." I took detailed notes and sketches—about three pages of them, in fact. The next morning, while driving to the experiment, I read my notes aloud to Stewart and told him what I thought the afternoon's video clip would be about. Unfortunately for my reputation as a telepath,[43] *I did the remote-viewing session the night before the experiment, a good fourteen or fifteen hours before the video clip was even selected.* I didn't read Stewart's mind at all—I didn't even try to read his mind. All I did was remote view the video clip. I imagined myself sitting just behind his shoulder watching the clip at the same time he did. Thus, I didn't read his mind. Instead, I watched the video with him. Of course, I watched it the night before the clip was actually played on the monitor—before the clip he saw was even selected by the computer.

As it happened, I was right.

Ganzfeld experimental protocols, and many other testing protocols in psychic phenomena, have a number of built-in assumptions about how telepathy and other psychic skills operate. A lot of these assumptions are, to put it gently, wildly and completely wrong, at least in my experience.

For example, there's the whole sender/receiver thing. This assumes that there is some kind of "something" that literally is *transmitted* between the person sending and the person receiving. The analogy is to radio, in which the person sending is the radio station and the person receiving is the radio itself. The problem with that is that in my experience, no such sender is required, ever. No one has to "send" anything. When you remote view something—and, I think, when you sense someone's state of emotions or state of mind—you don't "receive" anything so much as "tune in to" information that is already readily available. The trick is tuning in to the specific information you want to find out, but no one has to send it or otherwise transmit it. From my perspective, all such information is available all the time everywhere.

The other thing that some people might find a little off-putting about this particular experience is the whole issue of remote viewing the video clip the night before it was shown (and about one hundred miles away from the lab, I might add)— the night before it was even selected from the library of clips. How can this be? In a later chapter I'm going to revisit this whole time thing in more detail. For now, just be assured that one of the most difficult aspects of any test of psychic ability is that it appears to operate outside of normal time constraints. As described in chapter 3, it's as easy to remote view the past or future as it is the present. And as you'll discover later, time isn't anything like what we think it is. Whether we eventually discover that time is something we have all made up and agreed to treat as "real," or whether it's truly fundamental to the structure of the universe, the fact is time is downright weird. That weirdness means that experiments that seem to test events in the present may actually test events in the past—or the future. Remember that in Sheldrake's email experiment, the greatest success rate came at least ten minutes *after* the person sending the email was concentrating on the receiver of the email.

If you consider psychic phenomena from this perspective of all information being available everywhere all the time, a lot of the conundrums go away concerning how people know things instantly across vast distances of space (and time). If the information is already present at the psychic's location, nothing has to be transmitted, and therefore there's no difficulty with transmitting information faster than the laws of physics say it should be able to travel.

So my little foray into being a research guinea pig didn't demonstrate anything at all about my telepathic ability—or Stewart's either.[44] This is a consistent problem with telepathy experiments. Researchers often believe that because they think a protocol is intended to test for telepathy, the only explanation for a successful test outcome is telepathy. The fact is, many techniques may be used by participants in experiments. It's possible that some of the participants in this ganzfeld experiment may have used telepathy. But it's also possible that others, like me, were more comfortable using remote viewing or some other form of clairsentience (i.e., sensing from a distance).

The question is, does it matter exactly which technique people use to know what should be unknowable? Or is the most important thing simply the realization that it is entirely possible for ordinary folks to know things that are far beyond their five physical senses?

In fact, is it even possible to separate knowing by remote viewing from knowing by telempathy or telepathy? Are we splitting hairs by categorizing these as separate skills instead of recognizing that they are instead fundamentally the same thing?

Whether you call this telepathy or telempathy or remote viewing or some other form of clairsentience doesn't really matter as far as I can see. Whatever label you paste on these skills, they work—and they appear to work for most people, at least some of the time.

CHAPTER 5

The Fifth Black Swan: Animal Telepathy

So far, I've been talking about telepathic exchanges between people. Yet any pet owner knows that their pets often seem to demonstrate amazing telepathic intuition—and sometimes the pet owners believe they understand their pets' thoughts, too. For example, I have a cat named Tinkerbell, whom I've had since she was a tiny kitten. (Her photograph is shown here.) She's a Tonkinese, a breed created by crossing the Siamese cat with the Burmese, so she has a sturdier body than a typical Siamese but Siamese-like markings and points. In Tinkerbell's case, she's got a Champagne-colored body with lilac points on her face, ears, and tail.

In most surveys of cat breeds, the two most "talkative" breeds are the Siamese and the Burmese. So as a Tonkinese, Tinkerbell got lots and lots of genes encouraging her to chatter.

The result is that Tinkerbell is a "talker." She chatters at me all the time. She also plays favorites. There are certain friends with whom she particularly enjoys talking. What I find interesting is that when those people are on the phone, Tink will awaken from her nap (she's nearly always taking a nap), come downstairs (or upstairs) and insist on chatting with the person I'm talking to.[45] Now, this happens only for certain people, but not for others. If I'm talking to any of Tink's special people, she wants to chat with them. If I'm talking to someone else, most times she does not, though she occasionally may extend a brief greeting before going back to her primary occupation of napping.[46]

Clearly this is far from a scientific set of observations. It's possible that Tinkerbell notes subtle changes in my voice or other behaviors that inform her of the person on the other end of the line. Perhaps she recognizes the person's name when I greet them. Or maybe there are some other clues she senses that I don't, though that doesn't entirely explain her insistence that I call one of her special people. Still, her behavior is intriguing enough that I wanted to investigate whether research supported telepathy between people and animals as well as between people and other people.

As it happens, a surprising amount of very interesting research has been done on telepathic links with animals.

A question posed by Rupert Sheldrake some fifteen or so years ago is whether animals can know when their owners are returning home before there are any physical cues to the owner's return. This doesn't mean anticipating the owner's return once the car turns into the driveway. Instead, Sheldrake was talking about animals who show signs of waiting for their masters long before there are any cues possible—even when the master is in another city and just setting their intentions to head for home. Sheldrake's book, *Dogs That Know When Their Owners Are Coming Home: And Other Unexplained Powers of Animals* explores the concept of animal telepathy in detail.[47]

Who Is Rupert Sheldrake?

Rupert Sheldrake has impeccable academic credentials. He has a PhD in biochemistry and is a plant physiologist, with his doctoral degree from Cambridge University (Clare College), and a fellowship at Harvard University. Sheldrake is known as an iconoclast in biology and science in general due to his development of a theory of "morphic fields." This theory posits that an underlying field pervades the universe that controls the structure of developing organisms and other events. This theory, although controversial, offers an explanation for some otherwise difficult-to-explain observations.

The theory proposes that an embryo (or other new event or form) impresses its resulting structure onto the morphic field. Subsequent members of that same group tune in to the morphic field and adapt their structures to that previously established collective tendency. Their final forms, along with any variations on that collective tendency, feed back to the collective morphic field for that group, allowing for adaptation and modification of the structure over time.

Sheldrake believes these morphic fields apply not only to biological forms but also to inorganic structures. Thus, once a new crystalline structure is initially created, it is substantially easier to recrystallize it because that structure has been stored (via a resonance between the object and the morphic field) in the morphic field where it can be accessed by all future attempts to crystallize that substance.

Sheldrake's concept is that the morphic field is a universal one, underlying all aspects of physical reality. He also believes it applies to mental forms (ideas) as well, thus bearing some similarity to Plato's ideal forms.

So far, no one has devised a mechanism to test Sheldrake's morphic field theory scientifically, so it is currently highly controversial to mainstream scientists. Nonetheless, Sheldrake remains one of the most original and creative scientists in the world today.

Dogs are probably the easiest animals to do this type of research with because they tend to be natural people pleasers. They love when their owners come home and they happily anticipate their arrival. Many dogs get excited just before their owners arrive. What might explain that behavior?

One obvious answer is one of routine. If the owner arrives about the same time every day, clearly the dog may simply have gotten accustomed to that schedule. Nothing psychic about that! Yet, Sheldrake cites a substantial number of reports of dogs whose masters have highly irregular schedules, arriving home at a wide variety of times, and even from a variety of different directions. Yet these dogs somehow still seem to know when their masters are about to arrive.

Defining an Animal's Anticipation of Their Owner's Return

So how do we know that the dogs are anticipating a family member's arrival? Sheldrake notes certain common behavior patterns that are indicators of such anticipation:

- Animals may react prior to the owner's actual arrival by a fairly consistent time in advance, no matter what time the owner starts to journey home (i.e., irrespective of any schedule or habitual time of return); for example, the animal may start reacting five to ten minutes prior to arrival.

- Animals may react when the owner focuses his or her attention on arriving. For example, if returning on a plane trip, the anticipation may begin at the time the owner gets off the homeward flight.

- Some animals may react when the owner sets his or her *intentions* to leave for home, no matter how long that homeward journey lasts.[48]

Another obvious answer is that the dogs somehow smell, hear, or see something that cues them to their owners' imminent arrival. Smell clearly is relevant primarily for animals outside rather than inside a house or apartment with closed windows and doors. Yet while it might be possible for a dog to smell an owner coming if the arrival occurs within a minute or two of the dog's perception, it's an unlikely explanation for animals who begin to anticipate their owners' arrival by ten minutes or more.

Hearing, like smell, is also more acute in dogs than in people, so it may be possible that dogs are hearing the specific sound of their owner's car engine, for example. Yet for owners who live in big cities (New York or London, say), car commuting isn't an issue. These owners most often arrive by walking, and for those who live in high-rise buildings, the likelihood of even the sharpest-eared animal detecting their owner's return by hearing them arrive is inconsequential.

Sheldrake notes that dogs that anticipate an owner's return five minutes or less prior to arrival must be suspected of getting external cues to inform them of the arrival. However, when the animal starts reacting earlier than that, it may be that some form of telepathic action is happening. He has recorded well over one thousand examples of dogs behaving in anticipation of an owner's return on a consistent basis, and all three of the types of anticipation noted in "Defining an Animal's Anticipation of Their Owner's Return" are well represented in that sample. Furthermore, he has examples of animals who react to an owner's extended absence, such as an owner returning from an overseas assignment or extended holidays.

Sheldrake claims that his informal survey showed that somewhere between one-third and two-thirds of dog owners report some kind of anticipatory behavior on the part of their dogs. Based on this survey, he undertook a more formal telephone survey in four cities, two in very different areas of Britain and two in California (Santa Cruz and the San Fernando Valley, a Los Angeles suburb). The percentage of dog owners who claimed this type of behavior in their pets was remarkably consistent, at right around 50 percent.[49]

So if about half of all dogs react to their owners' arrival, why do the others have no reaction? Sheldrake proposes several possible explanations. First, owners who live alone have no way of observing if their dogs are reacting, so the behavior goes unnoticed. Also, if such anticipation was presented, but not reinforced by the owners, the dog may decide this was not acceptable or worthwhile behavior and will thus stop reacting. In addition, not all dogs and owners have strong emotional bonds. An indifferent owner likely would not generate an anticipation response in any dog. It is also possible that just as various skills vary in intensity in people, either individual dogs or possibly even specific breeds of dogs may be less sensitive to whatever psychic clues they use to anticipate an owner's arrival. Sheldrake, in his telephone surveys in Britain and California, also asked about the breeds of the dogs. Though no statistical significance was demonstrated for any breed, the toy breeds and nonsporting dogs showed responsiveness rates of about 65 percent instead of the 50 percent average. Again, while not statistically significant, it is an intriguing result because these breeds were bred in large part for companionship to people.[50]

In Sheldrake's survey of pet owners in California and Britain, the owners were also asked how their pets responded to the owners' *intentions* to leave. Specifically, the question asked was, "Would you agree or disagree that your pet knows you are going out before you show any physical sign of doing so?" In response to this question, two-thirds of dog owners and about three out of eight cat owners replied yes.[51]

So far, this is anecdotal evidence, but Sheldrake worked with some dog owners to provide detailed records of their dogs' behaviors over an extended period of time. One owner, named Pam, went so far as to videotape her dog when it was left alone at her home, and she asked her parents to log the dog's behavior when it was left in their care. She was also careful not to inform her parents of her expected time of return (and often did not know exactly when she would return in any event).

In eighty-five out of one hundred trials, her dog went to the front window to anticipate her return home at least ten minutes before she actually arrived. Furthermore, she noted when she made the decision to return home, thus starting a forty- to sixty-minute journey. Between 20 to 30 percent of the time, her dog started anticipating her return by going to that front window *at the time she made the decision to start home.* Except for those two time periods (when she decided to start for home, and about ten minutes prior to actual arrival), her dog was at that front window less than 10 percent of the time. These results are statistically significant.

Based on these data, Sheldrake set up a more formal test in which the front window was continually videotaped while Pam went out. She had a beeper with her, and at random times, she would be beeped; only then did she start for home. She also took a variety of different paths back to her home, and a variety of different transportation methods, including walking, driving, bus, and bicycle. Once again, her dog demonstrated very similar responses both to the times she set her intention to return (when she was beeped) and to the ten minutes prior to her actual arrival.

One of the obvious difficulties with research in animal telepathy is that it is challenging to interpret what they know against what they don't know, since few animals speak English. That is not true of *all* animals, however. Rupert Sheldrake worked with African gray parrot owner Aimee Morgana to test her gray parrot's ability to receive telepathic messages from her.[52] Morgana had noticed that the parrot, N'kisi (pronounced *in-key-see*), often seemed to respond to her telepathically, just as I have noticed Tinkerbell responding to me. (And, no doubt, as many readers have noticed in their pets, too.) The difference was that N'kisi had been trained to use language and was reasonably proficient at speaking. Morgana had seen television programs about Alex, a highly language-adept gray parrot, so she decided to teach N'kisi to speak when he was still a very young bird, just as she would teach a human child. By the time N'kisi was five years old, he had a functional vocabulary of seven hundred or more words and frequently made highly contextually relevant comments about events around him. By the time N'kisi was twelve years old, he had a vocabulary of fifteen hundred words, the largest parrot vocabulary ever recorded. He also started making comments on Morgana's *intentions* rather than observable events. N'kisi also started waking Morgana by making loud comments that directly related to the contents of her dreams in progress.

Sheldrake and Morgana designed an experiment to determine if N'kisi could actually read Morgana's mind. They took thirty words from N'kisi's vocabulary that represented items that could be pictured—things like "phone," "bottle," and "flower." A separate individual who was not present at the test selected a library of stock photographs from an online library that illustrated twenty of the thirty items; a total of 167 images were selected in all.[53] Each image was placed in a sealed envelope and shuffled and numbered. Twenty images were selected as "pretest" images to work out the kinks in the overall procedure, and the remaining 147 images would be test images.

One key is that neither Sheldrake nor Morgana knew what the images looked like, nor which vocabulary word was associated with each numbered envelope.

N'kisi was left in his cage in one room, with no one else in the room. Morgana was in a different room on a different floor. Both N'kisi and Morgana were continuously videotaped throughout the experiment. Morgana and N'kisi could not see or hear each other. During the experiment, Morgana said absolutely nothing, as was confirmed by the video recording. Thus, N'kisi could not receive standard sensory clues from either vision or hearing.

The test was conducted using a simple timer. Morgana opened an envelope and set a timer to beep after two minutes. During that two-minute period, she stared at the image. N'kisi was allowed to say whatever he liked during that two-minute period. Video cameras recorded what he said and did.

Of the 147 images, 1 was obscure enough that Morgana couldn't figure out what it was supposed to represent, so that image was immediately discarded. Ten images contained none of the selected vocabulary words and were eliminated. Four images had to be eliminated because they were photographs of cameras, which was in the vocabulary list but became a problem because N'kisi repeatedly mentioned "camera" in response to the cameras used to record the test results. A caller interrupted one image trial, so that was discarded also. The result was that there were 131 images in the final data set.

N'kisi's responses were transcribed independently by four different people, Morgana, and three others who did not know the targeted vocabulary words or the contents of the envelopes. These transcripts were then compared to the actual images and statistically analyzed in a variety of different ways. Depending on the specifics of the analysis, N'kisi's correct responses were judged to be more accurate than chance at odds ranging from four chances in one thousand to three chances in ten thousand.[54]

No matter how you slice it, this experiment clearly demonstrated N'kisi's ability to detect what Morgana was thinking with the likelihood of his abilities being true as significantly better than chance. (For comparison, in social sciences the standard acceptable confidence level is odds against chance of one in twenty; to achieve four in one thousand or three in ten thousand makes the results a near certainty.)

Parrots are very smart animals. They can learn to use language contextually at very advanced levels. While demonstrating a parrot's telepathy with its owner doesn't necessarily speak to the ability of a cat or dog to do the same, there are far more experiments with dogs and cats than with parrots.

What about other animals? Is animal telepathy limited to dogs, cats, and parrots? In a word, no. If we're limiting the discussion to animals that communicate with people, the one characteristic that seems to be required is a close emotional bond with the person. Interestingly, it may not be the case that the emotional bond with people is what *enables* the telepathic communication. Instead, it may merely be that without such a bond, the animal has no reason to *react* to knowing that their owner is returning.

Horses, like dogs and cats, often form close emotional bonds with their owners and riders, and there are many reports of them reacting in anticipation of the owner approaching them. While most often the behavior begins perhaps ten to fifteen minutes prior to the owner appearing, when the owner has been gone for a fairly long time, the anticipation can start a few hours before the owner arrives. Even when the humans around don't know that the person is on his or her way, the horse often is well aware of the imminent arrival and is waiting or exhibiting its usual welcoming behaviors.

A few chickens have been known to await the person who regularly fed them, even when the schedule of the person's arrival was irregular and not predictable. Even a goose or two have been known to eagerly await their owner, beginning their waiting only fifteen minutes or so before he arrived.

On top of that, an occasional sheep has been known to have a similar attachment to their owner, particularly those that have been hand raised since they were lambs. Sheldrake has also reported an occasional cow having such an attachment!

Other mammals are a bit more problematic. Sheldrake notes that he has no definitive reports at all of hamsters, gerbils, guinea pigs, rabbits, or rats reacting with anticipation, though he does have one report of a pet ferret. Though some reports exist, the response time is only a couple of minutes before the owner actually arrives, so the possibility exists that the animal may be hearing, smelling, or seeing some clue that gives away the owner's arrival. Sheldrake discounts these stories as "inconclusive."

As has been seen by N'kisi's story above, birds also can demonstrate anticipatory behavior. Within that category, Sheldrake reports that animal communications have been reported by owners of parakeets and cockatiels. In one set of trials with a woman in California who owned six cockatiels, the birds were videotaped continuously while she was away for random times at various times of the day (to avoid the issue of the birds getting used to a schedule). Again she was given a beeper, and at random times the beeper would tell her to return home. In seven out of ten experiments, the birds chirped more once she had decided to return home (a twenty-minute journey). Over the entire set of ten trials, the birds chirped 15 percent of the time during the period she was away from home, but more than three times as often, 49 percent of the time, during the twenty minutes she was on her way home. When statistically analyzed, these results were significant.

Sheldrake also notes that it is primarily birds in the parrot family that anticipate their owners' return—except he has noted that he has reports of one pet owl showing signs of knowing when its owner was coming home, and one pet mynah bird that would announce the name of the son in the family in the two or three days before he returned from overseas assignments—often returning without notice to the family.

All these animals are warm-blooded, yet Sheldrake has some data that indicates the possibility that certain reptiles sometimes anticipate their owner's arrival. One belly dancer who used a boa constrictor when she performed, and borrowed the snake from a local veterinarian, described the snake's behavior:

> Julian (the snake) spent many hours curled up next to me on my bed while I was studying and seemed to enjoy being taken out to participate in my dancing and visit with people in the audience. I always felt she and I had a mutual relationship based on affection. The secretary in [the vet's] office told me that every time I came to pick her up, about half an hour before I arrived Julian awoke from her deep snake sleep and started moving around her cage, sliding her nose back and forth across the cage door.[55]

Sheldrake has no reports at all of any pet fish anticipating their owners' return, in contrast to snakes, birds, and many mammals.

The evidence for animal telepathy is largely anecdotal, although Sheldrake's limited-scale trials with dogs and birds offer intriguing hints of the possibility of telepathy between animals and humans with whom they have strong emotional bonds. Designing well-controlled studies of animal communications with people is a daunting task, in large part because we cannot get testimony from the animals themselves (barring language-using parrots) and must infer their abilities from behavioral cues.

Another problem is that so far, psychic behavior has only been demonstrated (if only anecdotally) in animals with strong emotional bonds to one or a few people. Thus, a researcher cannot simply go to the local animal shelter, choose a likely looking dog or cat, and expect to get results. It requires the time and energy to allow the animal to become attached to an individual—and that means both the person and the animals have to be willing participants in the study. This also makes blinded studies challenging to design.

Yet, the anecdotal evidence that does exist makes compelling reading.[56] Any pet owner who has a close relationship with their animal may well recognize some of the features of animal telepathy Sheldrake is interested in. While I'm not yet prepared to claim that Tinkerbell is psychically attuned to my activities, I do know that she is sensitive to my mood and behaves appropriately to soothe and comfort me. That may (or may not) be a demonstration of any psychic skill, but it certainly shows an awareness of my emotional state.

The conclusion from this has to be that animals are extraordinary creatures whose behavior may prove to be far more complex and sophisticated than we now understand. It will take a very clever and dedicated researcher to develop a study design that will properly test these ideas. This is even more challenging when you recognize that you cannot simply perform the experiments in a laboratory. If Sheldrake is correct in his supposition that the key element for success is the existence of a close and strong emotional bond, designing experiments is not easy to do.

Science tends to shun effects that depend on emotional states for success. Perhaps that's the reason so few researchers make an active attempt to investigate these issues.

I have not addressed criticisms of Sheldrake's work in this chapter, in large part because the skeptics who have addressed this issue of animal communication have proven to be less than honorable in their claims against him. For some reason, the concept of animals being conscious, aware, and psychically capable seems to intimidate many people, including otherwise reasonable scientists. As a result, the criticisms of even the very preliminary studies Sheldrake has reported have sometimes been virulent far past the point of logic.

I will note just one instance of many as described by Sheldrake: an encounter with James "The Amazing" Randi.[57] I quote directly from Sheldrake's explanation of one specific instance with Randi.

> *In January 2000* Dog World *magazine published an article on the sixth sense of dogs, which discussed my [i.e., Sheldrake's] work. The author contacted Randi to ask his opinion. Randi was quoted as saying that in relation to canine ESP, "We at the JREF [James Randi Educational Foundation] have tested these claims. They fail." Randi also claimed to have debunked [the experiment with Pam's dog discussed above]. In* Dog World *Randi stated, "Viewing the entire tape, we see that the dog responded to every car that drove by and to every person who walked by."*

> *I e-mailed James Randi to ask for details of this JREF research. He did not reply. He ignored a second request for information. I then asked members of the JREF Scientific Advisory Board to help me find out more about this claim. They advised Randi to reply.*

In an e-mail on February 6, 2000, Randi told me that the tests with dogs he referred to were not done at the JREF but took place "years ago" and were "informal." He said they involved two dogs belonging to a friend of his that he observed over a two-week period. All records had been lost. He wrote: "I overstated my case for doubting the reality of dog ESP based on the small amount of data I obtained."

I also asked him for details of the tape he claimed to have watched so I could compare his observations [of Pam's dog's] behavior with my own. He was unable to give a single detail, and under pressure from the JREF Advisory Board he had to admit that he had never seen the tape. His claim was a lie.[58]

I believe that Sheldrake's explanation is totally credible.[59] Why? Because I have knowledge from other sources of the tactics used by Randi. As you may be aware, for many years Randi has had a million-dollar challenge, offering to pay a million dollars to anyone who can prove to his satisfaction that they have any paranormal power. Randi has gotten enormous publicity from the fact that no one has ever won this challenge in the many years he has offered it.

I'm going to put on my psychic hat and make another prediction: No one ever will win that challenge. It's an impossible one to win for any of a number of reasons. The first reason is pretty obvious: The person controlling payment of the money is also the judge to determine if the money is earned. Not much incentive for Randi to accept *any* proof as "sufficient," is there?

Worse than that, I have a friend who is an amazing psychic, and he actually applied for that challenge. Before he could be accepted to go for the million-dollar prize, he had to go through an increasing series of tests, and repeatedly, the criteria for the tests were changed as he accomplished more and more. In other words, Randi constantly changed the rules, the conditions, and the success criteria to ensure that anyone with genuine talent could *never* reach the point of actually taking the million-dollar challenge. In the end, disgusted with the blatant dishonesty of Randi's "selection" process, and realizing that anyone who demonstrated any real psychic talent would *always* be weeded out and not allowed to take the final challenge, my friend gave up.

There are two types of skepticism. One is the healthy skepticism that retains an open mind and considers the evidence fairly and without prejudice. That type of skepticism is good for science and for progress because it forces a search for increasingly better-quality evidence.

The other type of skepticism is the type displayed by the highly public "debunkers," many of whom, like Randi, have no actual scientific credentials but are willing to make any statement, tell any lie, and fake anything to dismiss genuine scientific evidence simply because they choose not to believe in the evidence in front of them. Unfortunately, in the past twenty or so years, this type of "evangelical" skepticism is growing and, in the process, damaging our ability to consider phenomena that may have vital importance to gaining a full understanding of the world.

Animal psychic studies are in their infancy, but Sheldrake's work provides an intriguing clue that our animal companions may be at least as capable of psychic skills as we are—at least that seems to be the case for animals that develop strong emotional bonds with people. In terms of those animals that do not develop such bonds, such as (apparently) fish and nondomesticated animals, they may have at least as much potential for psychic skills as our pet cats and dogs but simply have less motivation to use those skills in ways humans can appreciate. In any event, the evidence for this Black Swan is intriguing and worth pondering. Nothing is yet proven, but I can only hope that investigators will begin to study animal psychic behavior in depth.

CHAPTER 6

The Sixth Black Swan: Precognition

Did you ever wish you could know the future? If so, you might want to rethink—knowing the future isn't as wonderful as you might imagine. In fact, it can be downright disturbing—even scary.

A number of years ago, when I was taking my training in remote viewing, there was one exercise that smacked me flat between the eyes. As with the other remote-viewing exercises in that program, we were each handed a sealed manila envelope. This one had a person's first name (Betsy on my envelope), the name of a town (in my case a small town in California I'd never heard of), plus a date corresponding to a two-week period. I was taking this training in December, and the two-week period was the previous April, about eight months before my training program.

This was an exercise in remote viewing people for the purposes of healing. The people named on the envelopes had requested energy healing.[60] We were instructed to do our sessions as usual but to do them in two steps. First, we were to do our best to remote view the person named on our envelope, at the time period stated on the envelope, and diagnose their state of health. (I should note, this was a program in remote viewing, not healing, so many of us were not particularly experienced healers or medical intuitives.) In other words, we were to assess their condition not *now* but *at the time stated on the envelope*, again, in my case, eight months earlier. Once we had a sense of what was wrong, we were to attempt to imagine a golden "energy dolphin" and direct that dolphin to go to the person and do whatever healing was necessary, steering the dolphin to the places in the person's body we had detected needed healing. Then we were to retrieve the dolphin, come out of the session, and make notes on how we thought it went.

By this time, at the end of the week-long training program, we were pretty good at accessing that remote-viewing state, so the first part of the exercise seemed straightforward. Sure, we were looking into the past, not the present, but, by gum, if we could view locations all over the world, how much harder could it be to look back into the past?

Besides, after five sixteen- to eighteen-hour days in a row, we were too numb to protest.

Anyway, I retreated to a quiet place to do my session. As instructed,[61] I first tried to visualize what was wrong with Betsy, from that little town in California. Or rather, what *had been* wrong with her eight months earlier. In my session, I got an image of a stocky, middle-aged woman. It felt to me as if she had several problems. I got some joint pain in her knees, but nothing terribly important, just a bit of what my granny used to call "rheumaticky." I also got that she had cancer in one breast, and that it had spread to the lymph nodes in her armpit on the same side. But that wasn't her real problem. My sense was that her real problem was that she was terribly depressed. Partly it was because of the severe pain from the cancer, but it also was because of a sense of lack of support or connection to family and friends. So, my diagnosis of Betsy was that she had breast cancer that had metastasized to a limited extent, but with a lot of pain and severe clinical depression as a result. I recorded those notes and continued.

While still in the session, I began the next part of the instructions. Although when I do healing I don't often use the standard gold energy dolphin recommended by the program, in this case, I followed the directions given by the verbal guidance and sent a golden energy dolphin out to do some healing on poor Betsy.[62] When it came time to retrieve the dolphin (also standard procedure), however, I decided to do the exact opposite of the instructions.[63] Instead of retrieving the energy dolphin, I instructed it to stay with Betsy over the next two weeks (the period of time on the envelope) and continue the healing process. I recorded my notes of how the session went and what I had done.

Once I completed the session, I gathered my notes and my still-sealed envelope and trekked down to the gathering room to where the instructor waited. Once in the presence of the instructor, I was allowed to open the envelope. Inside were two pieces of paper. The first one was Betsy's request for healing. She said in that message that she had breast cancer that had spread to the lymph nodes in her arm. But that wasn't her most serious problem. Her greatest problem, she said, was that she was in severe pain, and the pain left her deeply depressed.

Wow. A perfect hit. For someone who didn't have any particular skill as a medical intuitive, I was impressed with such a perfect match between what I sensed in my session and what Betsy's actual physical problems were.

Then I looked at the second paper in the envelope. On it, Betsy had provided feedback on what she thought had happened in the two-week period she expected to have her requested healing. Her words were very clear: She felt better and less depressed, and her friends had noticed a difference in her attitude and that she seemed less in pain. But most of all, she felt as if *she still had a golden dolphin inside her healing her.* Furthermore, Betsy had written that report at the end of her two-week scheduled healing—*eight months before I actually did the healing session on her!*

When I read those words, I almost literally fell over. I had to sit down rather abruptly. I could discount her reports of feeling better because Betsy's own expectations could easily lead to a placebo-type effect where she convinced herself she was better in the time frame of her expected healing. That, in my opinion, meant precisely nothing about my effectiveness at anything, except perhaps that I had correctly diagnosed her condition in the first half of the session.

No, what shocked me to the core was her statement of feeling the dolphin still inside her. I tried to reassure myself that surely it was a coincidence. Since I didn't know all that much about healing, particularly back then at the very start of my psychic awakening, maybe it was common for people to leave the dolphins in the person being healed. Maybe it was *common* for people to feel the dolphins inside them and I'd just coincidentally happened to do that, even though that's the exact opposite of the instructions given us in the verbal guidance of the session. There are other folks who follow as instructions about as well as I do, after all. Maybe.

At our next big break, I wandered over to the office of the woman who ran the healing requests program. She has retired now, but I knew her pretty well, and I knew that since *all* the healing requests—and the feedback from them—passed by her desk, she would be the expert on whether leaving the dolphins in the patient, or sensing the dolphins being left in the patient, was common. I explained what I had done in the healing session. She said she thought that was a very clever idea. Then I asked if very many other members of the healing program did the same thing and whether other people who request healing report similar sensations. "Oh, I've never heard of anyone doing it that way before," she said. "Nobody ever said that before."

So there I had it. I had good reason to believe that in April, my healing efforts had been sensed by Betsy. Unfortunately, since I hadn't actually done the healing until December, there was a little problem. Either Betsy was looking into the future, sensing what hadn't happened yet, or I was looking into the past . . . *and changing it with my actions in the future.*

Either way, time was in trouble. Time suddenly wasn't flowing for me in one direction. It was flowing forward, the way it usually does as moment follows moment. But it also was flowing *backward*, allowing me to manipulate the past from the future, something that's a gigantic no-no in science.

Why is that such a problem? Here's the thing. There is one fundamental, almost always unspoken assumption that underlies all of science. That assumption is the bedrock on which all of science is based, whether it's chemistry or geology or biology or even psychology. The assumption can be stated in four simple words:

Causes come before effects.

If a scientist notices that two events occur together and if event A always happens before event B, and assuming there's good reason to believe A and B are related somehow, then the conclusion that she is likely to draw is that event A *causes* event B. In other words, if I take a hammer and use it to hit your toe, it's likely you'll say "ow!" Event A is me hitting your toe with the hammer. Event B is you saying "ow!" Since you won't say "ow!" until I hit you with the hammer, event A always comes before event B.[64] Thus, the scientific conclusion is that A *causes* B. My hitting your toe with the hammer *causes* you to say "ow!"

Seems a perfectly reasonable assumption, doesn't it? But now apply that same reasoning to my situation with Betsy.

Betsy is ill. I do a healing session on Betsy. Betsy says she feels better *and* she says she senses the *exact, idiosyncratic thing I did in the healing session*. She makes that claim spontaneously, without being prompted. It's just what she feels. Event A is my doing a healing session on Betsy, and event B is Betsy feeling the effect of that healing. Event A is the *cause*, and event B is the *effect*.[65]

Thus, the serpent in this little garden is the fact that in this instance, the cause, event A, happened in December, while the effect, event B, happened the previous April. At least for this specific case, cause did *not* follow effect. Instead, the effect came *first*, and only eight months *later* did the cause happen.

Effects coming before causes? That's just crazy.

In fact, it's so crazy that, if it's true and cause does not have to precede effects, *all of science is undermined.*

In that one moment, I realized that everything I thought I knew about the universe must be flawed. At least in some cases, under certain circumstances, causes do not have to precede effects. Time is not the unidirectional arrow that all of science assumes. At least sometimes, it must be bidirectional or maybe even (dare I say it?) flow in whorls and loops. And all of science comes tumbling down.

There is an alternative explanation that doesn't (quite) destroy causality. That explanation is that on that April day, Betsy caught a glimpse of the future. In other words, it's just possible that Betsy got a precognitive glimpse of something that would happen in the future. As a way of saving causality, this is, at best, a bandage, but it is slightly more palatable than turning the bedrock assumption of science into cottage cheese.

Whether you accept that causality has some serious issues, or whether you believe that Betsy was precognitive, either explanation implies some important problems with our current understanding of time, making it not as simple and linear and river-like as we would like to believe.

From my personal perspective, I have had enough experiences with weird time events since my working with Betsy that I now believe that time is a whole lot more complicated than that unidirectional arrow we all talk about. There's something funny about time. Maybe, in fact, that old punch line really is correct, and time is just something we made up to keep everything from happening at once.

In fact, maybe everything really does happen all at the same time.

Of all the psychic experiences I've had in the past decade or so, the ones that make me craziest are the ones where time is messed up. I sometimes experience strong fugue states where I do what I call "remembering the future." This is not the same as a déjà vu experience, where you walk into a room and it feels familiar for a brief moment. These are instances where I have strong, complex, and extended memories that I take as actual memories of incidents that haven't happened yet. When they do eventually happen, in fact, I get very confused because in my memory, they were experienced days—or months—before. Let me give you one of many examples.

My good friend Deb was attending a week-long retreat a year or so ago. During this retreat, we had very little contact, though I did briefly speak with her on the phone on Thursday night of that week. Friday was her travel day when she returned to her home in Canada, so the next time I spoke with her was on Saturday morning when she called to tell me about her week away.

At one point early in our conversation, she started to tell me about a peculiar dream she'd had the night before after she got home. I had to interrupt her. "You already told me about your dream," I said.

"No, I didn't."

"Yes, you did." Before this could degenerate into a "did not"/"did so" squabble, I gave her a detailed description of her dream, and what I had said in response, and what she had said in response to that, and basically laid out about ten minutes worth of conversation we'd had about the dream. I should note that I was *absolutely convinced* I had had this conversation with her as I described it.

Unfortunately for me, Deb was equally convinced I was wrong: "But I have *not* told you about the dream. *I just had it last night and I haven't talked to you since then!*"

Unfortunately for Deb, my description of her dream was dead-on accurate and the way I said she described it in our not-quite-real conversation was exactly how she'd planned to describe it to me that Saturday morning.

O-kay. That's when I realized that once again I was remembering a *future* event, not a past one. It wasn't the first time this had happened to me, nor was it the last. It just spontaneously . . . happens, at unexpected moments. When one of these events pops up, they are completely indistinguishable from regular memories, which is why I call them "remembering the future."

Frankly, they are not particularly pleasant occurrences when they appear because I find them deeply disorienting, as if I've somehow shifted to an alternate reality where what I think has happened hasn't—at least not yet.[66] They have led to a number of "vivid discussions" with friends when I insist things have happened when they haven't yet—but do happen later. To me they seem exactly like regular memories, not like predictions, so I can't distinguish between those future memories and past ones, something I find deeply confusing at times.

Moreover, these experiences pop up during daily life—not when I'm meditating or even necessarily right after I've meditated. They appear at random, without any warning, effort, or intention on my part. With that said, I can recall no instance of anything even remotely similar to this in my entire life—until I started meditating and developing psychically. That means I went through (mumble-mumble) decades of life with no similar experiences, only to now find it happens more and more.

Whatever the explanation for these events (and all the other similar ones), one thing has been driven home to me: Time isn't what we think it is. It's both accessible (past, present, and future) and malleable in bizarre ways. That's been my experience, and it still unsettles me. The question now is, does scientific evidence exist to support these experiences?

Lest you think that my experiences are sheer delusion, plenty of scientific evidence exists to support the notion that people can—at least sometimes—look into the future. Dean Radin presented a summary of peer-reviewed studies published in reputable journals that investigated the concept of looking forward in time.[67] Some of these effects were discovered more or less accidentally when testing for other things.

Radin's book is one I've mentioned before because he did a terrific job of assessing the scientific data on several paranormal phenomena. The data very clearly demonstrate the reality of the ability to look ahead into the future, at least over very short time spans. In addition to surveying other people's studies on the paranormal, Radin also is one of the best experimentalists in this field, conducting carefully designed and well-thought-out studies in a variety of paranormal areas.

In a typical experiment Radin conducted, participants sat in front of a computer screen. A series of photographs were presented on the computer screen one at a time. The subject was wired up with several types of physiological monitors to detect things like heart rate, skin conductivity (a measure of arousal), and the level of blood in her fingertips. The idea was to determine the degree to which emotionally arousing images changed her physiological state. Because people get inured to shocking or emotional images pretty quickly, the emotional-content-laden images (ones that were shocking, erotic, arousing, disturbing, or otherwise highly emotional) were interspersed among a large number of blander images with low emotional content (pictures of pretty landscapes, happy people, and natural scenes).

As Radin described the procedure,[68] the intrepid participant clicked a mouse when she was ready to begin. The mouse click started the monitors recording her physiological measurements. Only after that click did the computer randomly select an image from a large pool of emotional and not-so-emotional images to present to her on the screen. There was a five-second total delay between the time the participant clicked the mouse and the time the image selected was displayed on the computer screen. The image stayed there for three seconds, then the screen went blank for ten more seconds, resulting in a total of eighteen seconds of physiological measurements associated with each image, with the image presentation occurring in the sixth to eighth seconds of that period. Only after that complete eighteen-second period had ended could the participant click the mouse button to view the next image.

The timing sequence was important because it meant that the physiological monitors could synchronize the measurements of arousal, heart rate, and so on with the image presentation on the screen. A typical session consisted of forty different images, presented one at a time in these eighteen-second time blocks.

As might be expected, when shown the highly emotional scenes, the participants had a strong physiological response. Calming images showed no similar response. Nothing unusual about that. Also as might be expected since the time sequence was so fixed, participants' arousal systems started to activate in those five seconds before the image was displayed. Again, there's nothing all that interesting about that, except . . .

The strength of that pre-arousal anticipation was significantly stronger before images that were emotionally shocking than before the calm images.

In other words, participants knew whether to "brace themselves" before the disturbing images, or whether the image was not going to be disturbing so there was no need to prepare to be upset. They knew this—and their bodies physically responded—*approximately two seconds before the image appeared on the screen.*

Understand that when asked if they had any clue about whether the image was going to be emotional or not emotional, the participants consistently said they had no idea. This implies that our subconscious minds are a whole lot more clued in on what's going to happen than our conscious minds are.

Even more intriguing, when assessed by whether the emotional content of the image was highly negative (i.e., violent) or highly positive (i.e., erotic), the preimage responses were significantly different. In other words, not only did the participants somehow know when to prepare themselves for an emotionally arousing event, they also knew whether they should prepare to be shocked or aroused by that event. They knew at least something about the *content* of the image they were about to see.

Lest you think this is some kind of fluke, know that it has been replicated by several other researchers in other laboratories than Dr. Radin's with very similar results.

The point is that, at least unconsciously, we operate all the time with perceptions that are just a tiny bit ahead of the temporal curve. We are able to detect traces from events that haven't happened yet and prepare ourselves for those events. Granted, a two-second lead time doesn't amount to much, but if you're going to be running away from a cave bear or a marauding lion, having a two-second head start can mean the difference between being eaten or living to eat another day.

While my experiences looking ahead (and those of the many other people who have experienced at least flashes of precognitive perceptions) may not be explained fully by such a two-second subconscious look-ahead, the fact—and it is a *fact*—that we can look into the future even by two seconds should give great pause to anyone inclined to say that prognosticating the future is "impossible." That's simply not the case. Scientific evidence clearly demonstrates that it *is* possible—at least for the next two seconds, and possibly for the next two days . . . or months . . . or years . . . or even centuries.

One thing that is important to keep in mind is that most of physics is directionally independent with respect to time. For example, the basic laws of classical motion in physics can run either backward or forward in time. If you calculate the path of a cannonball, for example, you can do so either by starting at the point where it leaves the cannon and work forward to compute where it will land, or you can start at the point where it lands on your house and work backward to compute where the cannon must have been hidden in your neighbor's yard. In that sense, much of physics is time-direction independent. Neither moving from past to future nor future to past is preferred.

So let's consider the problems I have experienced with reverse-causation. Is it possible for cause and effect to switch places in the temporal stream? Is there any scientific justification for such bizarre events? You might think the answer would be no, but in fact, a better answer is . . . maybe. To provide further explanation of precognition and the issues of causality, however, we have to look more closely at the most successful physics theory of all time, one with equations that are completely independent of the direction of time. That theory is quantum mechanics.

Quantum mechanics is really unusual in physics. Generally speaking, physical theories arise because someone comes up with a metaphor or other analogy of the physical processes involved in a phenomenon. For example, the metaphor might say that the atom is like a solid ball of matter—it's an analogy between what we don't yet understand (an atom) and something we think we do understand (a solid ball of matter). Physicists held that analogy from the time of Democritus in ancient Greece until the beginning of the 20th century. In the 1890s some cracks in that analogy started to appear when J. J. Thomson discovered that the solid little ball of an atom maybe wasn't so solid—it definitely had subparticles in it, specifically the electron. That generated an analogy of an atom as being like an English plum pudding.[69] That in turn resulted in experiments to test that analogy.

When the experiments to test the current analogy are tried, the predicted results (based on the current analogy) are compared to the actual data from those experiments. When the data confirms the analogy, more experiments are tried to see how far that analogy can be pushed. How similar is an atom to a plum pudding?

As it happens, experiments testing the plum pudding model of the atom were actually done in the early 20th century, only a few years after that model was proposed. Unfortunately for J. J. Thomson's theory, the predictions did not match the data, so the analogy was proved wrong.[70] That meant that a new analogy had to be created. The old plum pudding analogy had to be replaced; the new one claimed the atom is like a miniature little solar system. That analogy appeared to explain the results from that first experiment and, in turn, led physicists to new experiments to see just how closely the atom resembles a little solar system . . . and so it goes.

That's the way physics generally works: Physicists think up an analogy or metaphor, develop some mathematics to make some predictions based on that metaphor, try the experiments and compare the results to the predictions, then modify (or throw out) the metaphor as needed to make more predictions.

But quantum mechanics is different. It didn't start as an analogy to something we understand. Quantum mechanics started out as a purely mathematical exercise in manipulating equations and was not particularly associated with any sense of how physical reality works. There was no metaphor to physical truth that guided the development of quantum mechanical mathematics. Thus, the mathematics of quantum mechanics is subject to *interpretation* in which metaphors that match the equations arc tried to see if they provide insight into what might be happening at a physical level. In other words, we know the mathematics works well, we just keep trying to understand the physical processes that make it work.

This is a bit like writing the mathematics of a recipe for a cake by first describing the final cake's qualities like texture, the height it rises, the flavor, and so on and then trying to match those qualities to specific ingredients, amounts of ingredients, and preparation techniques that might give those desired qualities to the final cake. The advantage in doing that for a cake recipe is that the possible ingredients and their properties are pretty well-known. An experienced cook might be able to do a "designer cake" based on an understanding of what the various ingredients contribute to an excellent cake. The problem is that on the quantum level, we cannot directly observe many of the "ingredients" and we may not even know what all of them are.

Quantum mechanics, starting out as pure mathematics instead of from a metaphor, needed to have some kind of interpretation of what the mathematics means in physical terms. The problem is, equations are really abstract—even for theoretical physicists. People—yes, even physicists—think about things more clearly when they have a metaphor to work with than when they deal solely with mathematics. The question then becomes, what do the symbols in the equations really correspond to in physical terms? What metaphor can we construct that makes sense physically but also corresponds to those equations? Constructing such a set of metaphors is called creating an "interpretation" of the quantum mechanical equations.

The most common interpretation of quantum mechanics is the Copenhagen interpretation, which arose from discussions (in Copenhagen, naturally) between Niels Bohr, Werner Heisenberg, and other physicists in the 1920s. This interpretation of quantum mechanics basically has a half dozen principles:

- To describe any event, you write its *wave function* to describe what an observer can measure about the event.

- Nature is fundamentally a set of probabilities, not hard matter. The probability of something happening—in other words, the probability that an observer can measure the event—is determined by the wave function that describes that event. When we observe an event, it (somehow) causes the wave function to collapse into a single point, which is the observation of that event. Exactly what the observer does to cause this collapse of the wave function from a wave to a point is unclear.

- It's impossible to calculate all the probabilities of all possible events because it's impossible to fully observe anything. There is always some degree of uncertainty in all measurements made by an observer.

- Matter, like light, is both a wave and a particle; how you choose to observe it determines whether it seems more wave-like or more particle-like.

- All our current ways of measuring anything can only really measure nonquantum characteristics of what they measure.

- When quantum-size systems are extended to the size of the regular world, the quantum description approaches that of classical physics. In other words, quantum mechanical effects are detectable only in the realm of the teensy-tiny and not in the world of ordinary life of the observer.

This is the interpretation of quantum mechanics taught in many (or most) colleges and universities, and if you've read even superficially about quantum mechanics, this is almost certainly the interpretation you find in the general press. It is the most common set of metaphors and similes applied to the quantum-mechanical equations.

This interpretation has some problems, unfortunately. There are issues in this interpretation in understanding what constitutes a measurement that (somehow) collapses a wave function—a cloud of possible realities—into a specific single value that gets measured by an observer. People also point out that the Copenhagen interpretation isn't very consistent because the "observer" part of the interpretation is not treated as a quantum system but as a classical physics system. Thus, it's unclear how the classical "observer" can influence the probabilistic quantum system being observed.

If this seems confusing, it's because, well, it *is* confusing. And inconsistent. And that's why there are other interpretations of the mathematics of quantum mechanics.

There are at least two other interpretations that may be relevant. One, called the "transactional interpretation," may lend insight to my problem with time.

The transactional interpretation was introduced by John G. Cramer of the University of Washington in 1986. In this interpretation of the mathematics of quantum mechanics, all events are sources (similar to light sources), and all sources emit waves that move forward in time. What is critical, though, is that all events also emit waves that move *backward* in time. Observers similarly emit both forward-moving and backward-moving waves through time. (Yes, they're supposed to be "observers," not "emitters," but the point here is that *everything* emits these waves all the time because the act of observing is itself an event.) Critical to this is the notion that these are *waves* traveling through time. Furthermore, these waves have the characteristic of all physical waves, in that they can cancel each other out if the crest of one wave arrives at the trough of another. To understand this, think of noise-canceling headphones. They create an equal-but-opposite sound waves to the noise from the outside to literally cancel out the sound of the noise.

So in the transactional interpretation, those forward- and backward-time-traveling waves sometimes cancel each other out, but they also sometimes reinforce each other, making the wave crest twice as high. This is fundamental behavior for physical waves. Once you say that something is "like a wave," this is the type of behavior you'd expect. It cancels out other waves sometimes, and it reinforces other waves at other times. They're a little like a clique in high school—they reinforce the waves just like them and cancel out waves that are their opposite.

The transactional interpretation of quantum mechanics assumes that the phases of these waves are such that once an observer perceives an event, it cancels out waves from the event that continue *later in time* and also cancels those parts of the wave that come *before* the event emits the wave. Thus, the only thing left that is detectable in time is the wave between the time the event emitted it and the time the observer received it. As it happens, that exactly corresponds with what we observe physically.[71]

Again, this is complicated (everything in quantum mechanics is complicated), but the point is that this interpretation assumes that everything emits waves that go both backward and forward in time, and that the only reason we don't see events before they happen (the waves sent backward in time) is because those waves are canceled out by other waves. In other words, in this interpretation, all events exist throughout all of time.

Thus, everything really does happen all at once, even if we cannot detect everything all the time.[72]

So, how does the transactional interpretation of quantum mechanics help to understand the problems with the cause coming after the effect? As has been demonstrated experimentally many times in the past ten or twenty years, quantum mechanics allows what Einstein called "spooky action at a distance." Such spooky actions means that objects that are entangled with each other quantum mechanically can affect each other instantly, even when they are too far apart for any information to flow between them.[73] This effect has been demonstrated across long distances (144 kilometers, or almost 90 miles, at the time of writing).

Such well-established nonlocal action implies that it might be possible to have communications that operate faster than the speed of light. If a way can be found to encode, say, the latest celebrity scandal and transmit it using such a scheme, we would all know the latest dirt at the same time.[74]

Cramer has described an experiment in which a signal sent from a transmitter to a receiver is received some fifty microseconds *before it is sent.*[75] The cool thing is that people have actually done experiments similar to Cramer's and found similar results. Most people are looking at this as a way to transmit information and possibly eventually objects faster than the speed of light—can you say, "warp drive"?

Physicists have tended to shy away from exploring the limits of causality, perhaps because the concept is so outrageous in contemporary scientific thinking. Sooner or later, however, someone is going to have to determine if causality really is all it's cracked up to be. In the meantime, the transactional interpretation of quantum mechanics gives a hint that causality's days may be numbered.

This is because nonlocality has an implication other than sending tweets faster than light speed and allowing message transmissions to approach the speed of rumor. It implies that it might be possible to *reverse the flow of causation.* In other words, it might indeed be possible, under certain circumstances, to have the effects come before the cause! Since, in this interpretation, all events exist throughout all of time, the "time" we assign to events is merely the time we observe it. Under special circumstances, therefore, it might be possible to detect events at different times than we do ordinarily. Remember that the observation of the event is itself an event, and that all events (even the act of observing another event) occur throughout all of time. Therefore, just maybe, there is a way to observe events before the time the event occurs.

The transactional interpretation of quantum mechanics is completely and fully symmetric with respect to time. Similarly, because the quantum mechanical equations are symmetric with respect to time, the transactional interpretation doesn't have the angst over nonlocality that is true of the Copenhagen interpretation. Thus the transactional interpretation of quantum mechanics could be compatible with the notion that perceptions of the future and manipulation of the past are all perfectly doable.

Symmetry in Time

Time symmetry in this sense means that equations work backward in time the same way they work forward in time. As noted earlier, classical mechanics are symmetric in time. You can compute the trajectory of a cannonball either backward from where it lands to where the cannon is that fired it, or forward from the cannon to where it lands. Similarly, the quantum mechanics equations work just as well moving backward in time as they do moving forward in time.

If this is the case, the implications are huge. The implications are that time isn't the simple linear flow we use as an analogy. It may be that we should dump that metaphor for time in favor of something very, very different. Or maybe, just maybe, we should eliminate the entire concept of time altogether. It's far too early to declare time passé, but there are enough straws in the wind, and enough instances of people being able to see and respond to the future, that, at the very least, we need to consider restructuring our mental metaphors for what time is and how it works.

Is that quantum mechanical breakdown of causality and nonlocality what I experienced with Betsy? It seems a stretch, quite honestly. Remember that quantum mechanics is assumed to hold sway only in the realm of the extremely small—at subatomic sizes. My experience was definitely in the macro world of the ordinary size. And yet . . . and yet . . . what cannot be ruled out as impossible must be accepted as at least possible.

CHAPTER 7

The Seventh Black Swan: Survival after Death

Almost fifteen years ago, my mother was dying. At the time, I wasn't quite sure of that fact, though I knew she was terribly ill, more ill than I had seen her in the years I'd looked after her in my home. This time, she was moving in and out of consciousness in a way that was truly frightening. She was bedridden and weak, but when she was awake, she was perfectly lucid.

I walked into her bedroom one morning, just as she awoke from sleep—or unconsciousness. She looked up at me and said, "Why are you here?"

I was immediately afraid that she had lost contact with reality. "I came to see how you are. Is there anything you need?"

"No," she said. "Why are you *here*? I'm dead. Are you dead, too?"

I had to swallow and take a deep breath before I could speak. "I'm not dead. You're not dead."

"But . . . " She looked a little confused for a moment. "Elmon was here. And Mike. And Uncle Willard and Aunt Martha and Mom. They were here talking with me. They were in the doorway. I must be dead. Are you dead, too?"

Elmon was my dad. He died in January 1972. Mike was my older brother; he died in November 1970. Uncle Willard had died long before I was born, and Aunt Martha, his wife, had died in 1968, two years before my brother. Uncle Willard had been a father figure to my mom, and he and Aunt Martha (my great-aunt) had been as much parents to my mom as her own mother, my grandmother. My grandmother ("Mom") died in December of 1972.[76]

These people were all people whom my mother deeply loved and missed. Despite that, never once, in all the decades since they died, had my mother ever expressed the slightest hint that she had seen or spoken with any of them. She was a very pragmatic and down-to-earth person, definitely not one given to spiritualist leanings. Also, she clearly understood at this moment that they were dead. She was not confused about that at all. Her only confusion was why *she* wasn't dead, too.

I could see that not only did she believe she was dead, but also she fully accepted that and was at peace with it. Her confusion and distress arose from her concern that I might be dead, too.

I didn't argue with her over her visions of people who had died long before, and as she came more fully awake, she didn't mention it again. Over the next few hours she was again slipping in and out of sleep. Later that day she was admitted to the hospital. Within twenty-four hours she was in a coma from which she never recovered. She died about ten days later.

But her announcement that she had seen and spoken to my deceased father, brother, grandmother, great-aunt, and great-uncle both comforted me and sent chills down my spine. As most people have, I had read accounts of people on their death-beds receiving visitations—or hallucinations—from previously departed loved ones. In fact, her announcement of that experience is what convinced me that she was dying and that she would not recover from this illness as she had from so many other setbacks in the past few years.

The problem was, I strongly believed at the time that there was no such thing as an afterlife. "When you're dead, you're dead," was my personal belief. Death wasn't terrible, nor was it heavenly. Death merely meant that you just . . . stopped. Nothing terrible in that, and certainly nothing to be feared, except, perhaps, for those left behind to carry on without you.

This concept of death as a mere cessation of being is the belief system that had been instilled in me through my training in physics, not to mention a career in one of the most down-to-earth, relentlessly logical fields out there: computers. In fact, my specialty was neural networks, computing systems that were physically modeled on the structure of the human brain. Working in neural networks, I was enamored with the concept that drives so many in the field: I felt that if we could make an artificial neural system complex enough, we would have made a brain—we would have made a *mind*. From my perspective the brain and the mind were identical, thus, when the physical brain shut down, so too did the mind cease to exist.

What this meant was that I had no philosophical system to fall back on to explain my mom's vision. In that respect, I was right in line with the beliefs of a substantial percentage of the scientific population today. Science is insistent that there is no afterlife, that it is impossible to survive the death of the body—actually, more specifically, that the mind cannot survive the cessation of brain function. Most of today's scientific investigations into consciousness and the mind start from the assumption that the physical brain and the mind are the same thing. Kill one, and you also kill the other. With such a set of assumptions, it is impossible even to conceive of the possibility that anything survives the physical death of the body.

As I write this, the Science Channel on cable television has a show called *Curiosity*. One of the first episodes of this show presented Stephen Hawking explaining why there cannot be a God or a Creator or anything like an afterlife. This was presented as scientific *fact,* mind you, not one person's opinion. Furthermore, the voice-over narration clearly implied that modern physics has completely ruled out any possible theory being true other than Hawking's conclusion. The show's point of view, like that of many scientists these days, was very much on the order of "Here's why all that supernatural stuff about God and life after death and such is mere superstition, but you can of course choose to believe in silly concepts if you like. Meanwhile, I'll simply consider you ignorant or dumb for believing in such childish myths."[77]

Yet when my mother told me about her vision of departed loved ones, I had seen the truth in her eyes. Whether I believed in an afterlife or not, for her, this was a genuine visitation from the dead. Furthermore, although I have never before admitted this to anyone, I caught a glimpse of those departed spirits, too— and I felt their presence in the room. I knew they were there.

I can't say that this one event completely changed my opinion away from that "when you're dead, you're dead" perspective. I was all too willing to let myself discount my own perceptions and instead believe that I simply imagined those spirit presences in my mother's room that day. Yet my mother's passing marked a sea change in my life that, within a couple of years, led me to question that scientific materialism view of how the universe works.

I've now had enough personal experiences communicating with the dead under circumstances that are sufficiently convincing (to me, anyway), that I've taken a U-turn in my belief system. I still don't "believe" in an afterlife—now I *know* for a fact that it's true. There *is* an ongoing existence after the physical body dies, even if it's not exactly like any of the major religions describe.[78]

Yet my personal conviction that this is true is only my personal opinion—just as Stephen Hawking's is his personal opinion. It won't convince anyone else of anything. The issue once again is whether credible scientific data exist to support the existence of life after death. As it turns out, not only does such scientific evidence exist, but also it's extremely credible.

What was it that my mother saw on her deathbed? Was it a true vision of those who had died decades ago? Or was it merely a hallucination? One scientist at California State University, Bakersfield, L. Stafford Betty, investigated deathbed and near-death visions in an attempt to answer that question.[79] Betty considered two types of visions. The more common vision is much like the one my mother had. In this case, the dying person sees spirits, generally of relatives, friends, or other loved ones who have died before. These spirits are seen to come to greet the dying person and encourage them about the positive nature of their coming transition from life to death. The spirits are nearly always recognized by the one dying but are not generally observed by others in the room at the time.

The second type of deathbed vision is something like a travelogue in which the dying person is given a glimpse of a wonderful place that they know is where they are going after they pass into death. Often, these visions occur only moments before death, and the words spoken by the dying are obscure and somewhat uninformative: "It's so beautiful there!" is a typical utterance for this type of vision.

Betty also noted that these visions can happen under two types of circumstances. One is when people are dying over a period of time, as from a major illness; this was my mother's situation. In these cases, the visions happen any time in the days or weeks before physical death, and the person is often conscious immediately after or even during the vision. People who are conscious when experiencing this type of vision see both any living people present and the dead at the same time and can communicate with both. (Thus my mother's concern about seeing and speaking to me at the same time as speaking to her dead loved ones.) They also generally know the difference between the living and the dead, though they sometimes count themselves as among the dead, as my mother did. The dead generally appear as "spirits," while the living appear as normal people.

The other circumstances of deathbed visions are those who are in perilous circumstances that may or may not result in imminent death. These latter often turn into classic near-death experiences where they may be given a choice over whether to return to their bodies—or may be ordered to return to their bodies. In such circumstances, the individual can generally offer comprehensive descriptions of their experience once they recover.

Betty provides four reasons why these reports should be taken seriously as valid anecdotal reports of the existence of spiritual survival after death. First, he claims that the dying person reports them as being visions of "living" spirits—even when they are die-hard atheists and materialists with no prior belief in an afterlife. They also tend to be very adamant about the reality of their experiences—again, no matter what their prior beliefs in survival after death. Unless you're willing to denounce all such deathbed claims as totally delusional or flat-out lies, you have to admit the possibility of at least some of them being accurate representations of what was experienced.

Second, Betty reports that the visions reported are those of people who are *deceased*. It is not a hodge-podge of random people from the person's life experience all jumbled up as hallucinations are. Instead, only those who are actually dead appear in these visions as spirit beings.[80] In other words, when the dying person sees both living people in the room and the spirits of the dead, they can distinguish the living and the dead. These death-bed visions simply don't have the randomness characteristic of hallucinations.

The third reason Betty presents for the reality of deathbed visions is that it has been shown in Europe that near-death experience happen when the brain has flatlined. In other words, the brain has completely shut down—and that's when the near-death experience happens. In fact, not only has the cerebral cortex (the thinking part of the brain) shut down, but so too has the brain stem, which handles autonomic functions. In other words, these people have *no brain function* at the time of the near-death experience. (Clearly, the report of the near-death experience happens only after the person is resuscitated and returns to conscious-ness.) Thus, the near-death experience cannot be a function of the brain shutting down, as many skeptics claim, because the brain has *already* shut down at the time the near-death experi-ence occurs. Yet despite the lack of brain function, those having these experiences perceive themselves as existing out of their bodies, able to see and hear what is going on around the physi-cal body below them.[81] If the brain is shut down, it cannot also be generating hallucinations—hallucinations require an active brain function.

Finally Betty points out that there are hundreds of validated reports of those who have a near-death experience who report discovering information during the experience that was well outside their physical perceptions, yet which was later deter-mined to be completely true. Clearly people experiencing near-death experiences are still able to observe the world around them, not only in the room where their physical bodies are, but also in other locations, too. Again, hallucinations do not gener-ate accurate information about the physical world.

One potential weakness in these arguments is that some-times near-death experiences, particularly those of children, and as opposed to deathbed visions, do include people who are still alive, and sometimes have elements that seem metaphorical. For example, one little girl chose to return to her body by press-ing one of two buttons: a red one would allow her to stay in the afterlife (to die) and a green one would return her to her body (to live). Another five-year-old reported sitting on the lap of God and being told he could not stay but had to return to his body.

Perhaps the most reasonable explanation for this type of near-death experience report is that as a whole they are inde-scribable. People can only report them in terms of their life experiences. So in trying to describe the indescribable, it is easy to understand how children in particular can explain their deci-sion process in terms of "pressing a button" or being comforted on God's lap and being told they had to return.

One thing I have learned about not just the afterlife but also all psychic states is that they are fraught with metaphorical and symbolic representations. Whereas a hallucination is made up out of nothing except the random firings of neurons, a spiri-tual vision is an attempt to make sense of perceptions that are beyond our physical experience. It is as if an ancient Egyptian were shown an iPad. What sense would he make of that? Prob-ably, it would be called something on the order of "magical papy-rus" because the concept of a wireless computer pad would have no meaning for him. Our minds cannot necessarily grasp the reality of a spiritual world so much vaster than physical reality, so we convert our perceptions into metaphorical ones that make sense to us.

If we accept that it's possible that some part of us survives death, the next question is whether there is some way to perceive that, or to communicate with that deathless part of ourselves. In other words, do psychic mediums really communicate with the dead, or are they all simple frauds and cold-readers, as skeptics claim?

What Is a Cold-Read?

One of the common claims by skeptics is that mediums get their information by "cold-reading" the person they're doing the reading for. This is, in fact, a common technique used by magicians and other stage performers when doing a "psychic reading" for an audience volunteer. For example, the magician may say something like "I'm getting an older male, whose name is C-something. C- Ch- Ch- . . . " Meanwhile the volunteer, all excited, blurts out: "That's Uncle Charlie!" The magician instantly stretches his response to "Char- Charles? Does that make sense?" The volunteer immediately agrees, perhaps volunteering more information: "He died in a plane crash." At this point the magician says something like "I have a sense of falling. Does that make sense?"

In essence a cold-reading basically is a subtle way to trick the person you're doing the reading for into revealing the information that you then turn around and "reveal" as coming from good old dead Uncle Charlie.

The problem with this assertion is that the skeptics make such claims even about testing protocols in which the subject of the reading *says nothing at all.* Nor can the psychic reader be reading body language, because in well-designed protocols, the reader cannot see the subject of the reading. In many of them, the reader and the psychic aren't even in the same state because the readings are conducted over the telephone.

One of the most studied forms of communication with the afterlife is the near-death experience, in which people are brought very close to death and in fact to actual physical death (as shown by the flat brain scans during near death experiences)."What Are the Common Characteristics of a Near-Death Experience?" describes the array of common characteristics that may be experienced.

The International Association for Near-Death Studies reports that near-death experiences, whether positive or negative, do not correlate in any way to religious beliefs, age, gender, sexual orientation, race, behavior, life experiences, economic status, or reasons for being brought to the brink of death. In addition, for those who do have a near-death experience, none of these factors are indicative of whether the experience will be joyful or terrifying.

What Are the Common Characteristics of a Near-Death Experience?

Near-death experiences are unique to every individual, but there are common characteristics that frequently appear. About 85 percent of them are peaceful and loving, and about 15 percent are frightening. Common characteristics, defined by the International Association for Near-Death Studies (*www.iands.org*) include the following:

- The presence of extremely intense emotions, usually ones of peace and love, but sometimes ones of fear.

- The sense of being above one's physical body, looking down on it. There may also be a sensation of moving to a different location. Commonly, the person observes medical efforts to resuscitate him.

- The sense of moving rapidly through darkness (sometimes a "tunnel") and often toward a bright white light.[82]

- The sensation of being in a different place—"somewhere else"—in a place that appears to be a different, sometimes spiritual world.

Continued

What Are the Common Characteristics of a Near-Death Experience? (continued)

- The sense of being intensely alert and able to think rapidly and efficiently.

- The experience of meeting with deceased loved ones, and other spiritual beings that may not be recognized, but with whom the person can communicate. While the communications are usually peaceful and loving, in some cases, the communications are terrifying.

- The sense of reviewing one's life history, seeing every event, both good and bad, and feeling the emotions of those events.

- The sense in some cases of receiving vast amounts of knowledge or understanding about the universe.

- The sense of being offered a decision of whether to return to the body or stay in spirit; in other cases, being told that "it's not your time" and being directed to return to the physical body.

Most commonly, about 80 percent of the time, near-death experiences are *transformative*. They change the life of the person who goes through it, generally forever. The most commonly reported transformation is the complete loss of all fear of death.

Although these are the common characteristics, no individual experience is likely to have all these characteristics.

The prevailing assumption of scientific investigations of near-death experiences is that they are a direct result of the shut-down of the physical brain. Elaborate explanations have been offered about how various chemicals released into the dying brain can somehow generate a set of common hallucinations that are interpreted as the near-death experience. Other experimenters have tried to reproduce the experience by using drugs or by stimulating specific areas of the brain. Let's take a moment to consider these explanations.

Probably the most commonly touted "explanation" for near-death experiences is that they are the result of a lack of oxygen to the dying brain—anoxia. The problem is that the characteristics of anoxia don't really match the characteristics of near-death experiences. In anoxia, people are highly disoriented and have very poor memory, effects that are the opposite of a near-death experience, where the experience is generally remembered vividly.

Another explanation sometimes offered is that certain chemicals—some of them naturally occurring in the body—generate experiences "just like" near-death experiences. These include drugs like ketamine and psilocybin as well as certain hallucinogenics. The difficulty again is that there's no correlation between the presence of such drugs in the body and near-death experiences. The drug may simulate some aspects of a near-death experience, but near-death experiences cannot be caused by drugs that are not in the body.

A third explanation commonly offered is that electrical stim-ulation of various lobes of the brain in the laboratory can gener-ate experiences that resemble some aspects of the near-death experience. Investigators who stimulate areas like the hypo-thalamus, the hippocampus, the frontal lobe, or the amygdala can cause their subjects to have some sensations that resemble a near-death experience. However, there are two major problems with this as an explanation for an actual near-death experience. First, none of the experimenters have been able to produce a syn-drome of experiences that match the array that an actual near-death experience entails. But more importantly, in a flatlined brain, it's hard to image what is stimulating the various parts of the brain and thus generating the symptoms.

Still not convinced? If you want an in-depth, detailed, and definitive discussion of the evidence for the reality of near-death experiences as something other than the result of random chemicals or electrical impulses in a dying brain, I can recommend nothing better than Chris Carter's book *Science and the Near-Death Experience*.[83] Carter reviews all the "scientific" explanations for near-death experiences and offers detailed explanations for why each is inadequate.

More than that, though, there's a fundamental fallacy that pervades scientific investigation of the near-death experience (and many other psychic issues). Simply because you can *simulate* a similar effect via drugs or electrical stimulation or any other technique does not in *any* way imply that those techniques are what happens in the real experience. I like to explain it like this. Suppose you walk into the cockpit of an airplane in New York's Kennedy Airport. You settle into the pilot's seat, run through your checklist, and take off. As you look out the window, you see ground moving below you and you fly to, say, San Diego. Once at the West Coast, you contact the control tower and land your plane. When you have the plane successfully shut down, you leave the cockpit. Where are you?

Well, if you were *truly* flying a plane, you're at San Diego's Lindbergh Field. Yay! Go have a great time in one of America's most beautiful cities! However, if you've been "flying" in a flight simulator based in, say, Omaha, when you walk out of the cockpit . . . you're still in Omaha. The simulator gave you a *simulation* of a real flight from New York to San Diego—but at the end of the experience, you're still in Omaha. Only the real thing results in being transported across country to San Diego.

Demonstrating that some characteristics of an experience can be *simulated* by drugs or electrical simulation or any other means in *no* way implies that the real experience is accomplished that way. As my magician participant told me, it's perfectly possible to *simulate* bending forks using magic tricks, but when you do it in actuality, it's a whole different experience.

It always shocks me when scientists—very smart people, who supposedly know the difference between a simulation and reality—claim that because they've re-created this or that individual symptom of a multifaceted experience, it means they've found out how it "really" happens. That's simply a completely ridiculous misuse of logic.[84] Only if you study *actual* experiences can you begin to understand what's really happening in them. Simulations that only generate one or two of the characteristics of the total experience are merely simulations. If a scientist can't distinguish between a simulation of an experience and an actual experience, of what value are his or her conclusions?

Truthfully there are techniques that appear able to generate experiences virtually identical to near-death experiences (without the death part). These include certain mystical traditions such as yoga, deep meditation, shamanic drumming, and other similar processes. In my experience, I have found that meditation does work and does generate experiences that cannot be distinguished from the near-death experience, complete with virtually all the characteristics noted as typical of near-death experiences.

My personal experience is that the truly mystical experiences are transformative. Once you begin to have them, your life is significantly changed *forever.* You can no more go back to the person you used to be than you can sprout gills and turn into a fish. Any experience that results in only one or two of the syndrome that correlates with near-death experiences and that does not result in a transformation of the person is merely a fake version of the experience. Fakes are interesting, or even fun. But they don't actually move you from New York to San Diego.

The problem, of course, is that studying psychic experiences in a laboratory requires extremely clever experimental protocol design. Some of the best-designed scientific studies of mediumship—the ability of talented psychics to communicate with the dead—have come out of the University of Arizona. Beginning with Gary Schwartz in the late 1990s and continuing with students trained in that tradition, intriguing studies have repeatedly produced excellent-quality data in support of the survival of consciousness after death. Critical to these experiments is that each participating medium is allowed to use their own individual techniques in environments they are personally comfortable with. This is accomplished in general by doing the readings over the phone, with the medium in their own home environment.

Doing the experiments by telephone also ensures that the psychic cannot use body language of the sitter to "cold-read" the sitter or the deceased. In fact, in most of the protocols, the sitter isn't even on the phone conversation at all. Instead, the experimenter—who knows only the first name of the deceased person but not other details about the person—sits in as a "proxy" sitter. Thus, *no one* on the conversation has any prior information about the person being read.

In these tests a variety of testing protocols were used, but a typical test might go something like this.[85] The medium is in his or (usually) her home in city A. The person receiving the reading (the "sitter") is in his home in city B, usually in a different state. The experimenter is in the city of their work, city C. The deceased person who is the target of the reading is, of course, wherever deceased persons are, if anywhere. Most commonly, all three cities are in different states. The experimenter knows the deceased person's first name, but no other information about the departed loved one that is to be read. There is a list of specific questions about the deceased person that the medium will be asked to answer by communicating with that person's spirit.

The medium's answers to the questions are recorded, and after the experiment is over, the responses are sent to the sitter for scoring. Schwartz developed a highly detailed scoring process, carefully described in his book *The Afterlife Experiments*.[86] In extensive tests of talented mediums across a number of years, the accuracy of talented mediums in answering such questions (along with other details and information) was typically in the 75 to 95 percent range. In contrast, a control group of nonmediums typically scored 25 to 35 percent accuracy.

What Kind of Information Do Mediums Receive?

Researchers from the University of Arizona mediumship studies ask mediums questions about the dearly departed such as the following

- What did the deceased person look like in life?

- What were the deceased person's personality like?

- What was the deceased person's favorite hobbies or activities?

- What caused his or her death?

- Are there any questions or messages from the deceased person for the sitter?

As noted in *The Afterlife Experiments*, in a number of cases, information was provided by the mediums that not even the sitter knew about. Such information had to be researched after the reading to confirm its validity. The bottom line is that Schwartz and the other researchers from his laboratory have demonstrated that some type of communication with departed loved ones appears not only possible but also likely. The care taken to ensure scientific validity of these experiments is impressive, so much so that it is difficult to arrive at any other explanation other than that the mediums really did communicate with the spirits of departed loved ones.

If all this evidence is out there, why are so many mainstream scientists hostile—often actively hostile—to the concept of life after death? David Fontana presented a very cogent explanation for this phenomenon.[87] He presents several interrelated reasons for this. First, many scientists seem to believe that if the mind or spirit or soul exists even after the physical body dies, it will require a complete revision of all the laws of physics and nature. The same belief holds for their worry over admitting that psychic phenomena are real. In other words, they are afraid that the walls of scientific orthodoxy will come tumbling down around their ears if they admit either a nonphysical aspect of our being or the reality of psychic phenomena. Yet this is not the case at all. Acknowledging that we all have souls, for lack of a better term, in no way negates the power and efficacy of quantum mechanics or the validity of electromagnetic theory. Instead, the reality of a soul and psychic abilities merely pushes at the edges of where current scientific theory no longer applies. They show us where we have more work to do to understand the workings of the universe.

A second reason Fontana claims that today's scientists deny the existence of an afterlife is that they say this is a question that is inappropriate for science to study at all. This argument insists that the afterlife is a matter of personal belief, not of credible fact, and therefore science can have nothing to say on the subject.[88] Yet, as has been seen in the studies discussed in this chapter, that argument isn't valid. It *is* possible to do well crafted, highly enlightening experiments on the afterlife. Furthermore, while controlled experiments are one way science grows in understanding, personal observations and anecdotal evidence are also credible evidence, particularly when such reports number in the thousands or even tens of thousands and arise from people who receive no personal gain from making such reports. That too is characteristic of the evidence of the existence of the afterlife via the near-death experience reports. To throw away so many reports that are so consistent, from all cultures and economic statuses, is akin to throwing away all the evidence that an object falls to Earth when you drop it simply because you don't yet have a credible theory of gravity.[89]

Another reason Fontana presents for the rejection of the afterlife and many psychic phenomena is that academic parapsychologists (i.e., those with respected and recognized credentials) are terrified that doing experiments in the field will result in the utter loss of credibility they have built up so painfully over the last seventy or so years. Parapsychologists already "don't get no respect" in academia, and to go out and investigate poltergeists, ghosts, mediums, or spirit communications in the real world threatens to turn them into complete laughingstocks within the academic community. It's too big a professional risk for most scientists to take.[90]

Yet another reason Fontana provides for shoving investigations of the afterlife onto the back burner comes from organized religions. Nearly all major religions have a vested interest in keeping the voice of authority within the halls of the priesthood or church hierarchy. If ordinary people have access to psychic skills, if they can visit the afterlife and return via near-death experiences, that undermines the authority of the church to tell people How Things Really Are. The result has been a consistent demonization of psychics across the centuries and a not particularly well-hidden complicity with the halls of science to denounce any hint of acceptance of psychic phenomena, communicating with the dead, speaking with spirit beings, or any similar event.[91]

To complicate matters even further, as a society we are, at best, death phobic. I see this all the time. Everything in our society today is focused on staying alive as long as possible. Our medical system isn't so much about providing the best possible care as it is about keeping the heart beating for as long as possible, often far beyond any possibility of useful recovery.[92] We are so afraid of dying that we refuse to acknowledge that it is a natural part of living a quality life.

How much easier would it be to face death, either our own or that of a loved one, if we *knew*—not believed, but *knew* from direct personal experience—that death really is nothing but a transition to a life free of physical pain and suffering? Would we be so frightened to let go if we *knew* we would be able to communicate with departed loved ones even after their physical bodies had turned to dust? Such knowledge brings serenity and acceptance of death. In fact, one of the greatest gifts from learning to understand our psychic selves, in my opinion, is that you lose the fear of death that so pervades the Western society. Yes, it is sad to lose the physical presence of a loved one, but it's not as tragic as it would be without that knowledge. Yes, we have reason to grieve over the loss. But it's far less devastating to lose someone you love if you know that the person survives in spirit than it is to believe they are forever out of reach.

CHAPTER 8

The Eighth Black Swan: Reincarnation

Sometimes I think my cat Tinkerbell is the reincarnation of my mother.

You see, my mom was what is politely known as an "early bird." Probably her habit of rising before the sun was up arose strictly from a lifetime of necessity because she worked full–time and had three rambunctious kids, a husband, and a house to look after. That's not to mention two elderly relatives living with us throughout my childhood: her mother, in her seventies then eighties with Alzheimer's, and her Aunt Martha, about ten years older and physically frail, though not, thank God, with any mental deterioration. With all that going on, and an extremely limited budget, getting up early and going to bed late was a necessity rather than a preference.

The problem for me was that, like many in their teens, my biological clock was a little different, and I wasn't crazy about getting out of bed at 6:00 a.m., seven days a week. (Yes, week-ends were devoted to house-cleaning and chores, so they weren't exempt from that early-to-rise dictate.)

My mother didn't let up on that early-morning schedule even once I was off to college. I well remember one specific

Thanksgiving my senior year. This was after my father, brother, and great aunt had all died, and my grandmother was (at last!) living in a nursing home, so my mom had the whole house to herself. I think she found it a bit lonely. On this particular Thanksgiving holiday, I had an exam that lasted until about 5:00 p.m. on Tuesday. I had loaded my car with my luggage, and once the exam was over, I got in and started the eleven- or twelve-hour drive from Connecticut to the Cleveland suburbs, driving straight through the night. By the time I got home around 5:30 a.m., I had been up about twenty-four hours. My mother knew exactly what time I arrived home because she was up when I got there—hey, it was nearly 6:00 a.m., right? Of course she was up!

I spoke with her briefly, pulled my stuff from the car, went to my bedroom, and collapsed into sleep around 6:30 a.m.

At 9:00 a.m., I was awakened by my mother rapping at my door. "Are you going to sleep all day?" she asked.

Well, actually, sleeping a little more than two or three hours *had* been part of my personal plan for the day, but any hope of accomplishing that had now evaporated. Dutifully, I got up and stumbled through the rest of the day.

So why do I sometimes wonder if Tinkerbell might be my mom? It's because Tink is an early riser, too. An *insistent* early riser. No matter how late I stay up working, she not only supervises me, so she knows exactly when I go to bed to sleep, but also—just like clockwork—come 6:00 a.m., she's squalling at me: "You gonna sleep all day, minion?"[93]

Yup. That's my mom, all over again.

I'm joking of course. (At least I think I am!) I do not *really* think that my mother reincarnated as my cat.[94] But as noted in the previous chapter, if we survive death, as evidence demonstrates we just might, is it possible that we also can reincarnate—come back as another person to live a whole new life?

Probably everyone recognizes that reincarnation is a significant part of the belief structure of some major world religions. Hindu Jainists, Buddhists, Sikhs, and followers of some sects of Islam[95] all include reincarnation as part of their religious beliefs. This means that at least one person in three in the world comes from a tradition that includes reincarnation. While it may seem strange and exotic in the Western world, in other parts of the world it is a perfectly normal and acceptable belief.

Many people in the West believe in reincarnation despite not being affiliated with any Eastern religion that includes that as a tenet or having New Age beliefs. A 1999 survey in Britain looked at people in the general public who believed in reincarnation.[96] The researchers concluded that not only was belief in reincarnation rising throughout their survey population, but also that it coincided with the increasing tendency of Westerners to "privatize" their religious beliefs. That means that people tend to want to decide for themselves about issues that their "official" religious affiliation does not include or about which they, as individuals, disagree.

A much more recent study associates belief in reincarnation with several dimensions, including what happens to personal consciousness after death, what happens to personal identity and personality after death, and what happens to the physical body after death.[97] In other words, they broke down belief in reincarnation into those three areas rather than asking a simplistic "do you believe in reincarnation?" type of question. The thing is, believing in "reincarnation" isn't a simple "yes I do"/"no I don't" question. There are all sorts of variations on the belief in reincarnation as shown in the figure, which illustrates the dimensions of measurement of reincarnation belief explored in this study. In particular, they looked at whether the participants believed that any part of themselves would survive physical death (i.e., annihilation or survival), whether they would survive with or without conscious awareness, whether their personal identities would survive, and whether they expected to have a physical body or be solely a spirit entity after death.

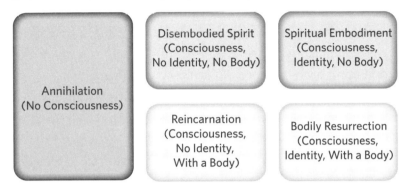

Students at a North American university were polled on their specific beliefs about what happens after death compared to their stated religious preferences (Protestant, Roman Catholic, Muslim, Hindu, Buddhist, Personal Religion, Agnostic, or Atheist; so few respondents in this study listed Judaism or "Other" as their affiliated religion that those groups were ignored in the study). Interestingly, although there were some stated religious affiliations with reincarnation beliefs consistent with that affiliation, many other people held beliefs about postdeath fates that were substantially different from their stated religion's official perspective. One of the chief effects was a huge schism between a materialist world view, in which the expected fate was "Annihilation" in the figure, and those who held a faith-based world view. Atheists and (to a large extent) agnostics almost universally embraced Annihilation as their ultimate fate. Hindus were most apt to express a belief in reincarnation. Christians (whether Protestant or Roman Catholic) expressed a very low belief in bodily resurrection, despite this being a tenet of Christianity as stated in the Apostle's Creed and the Nicene Creed.

The point here is that we believe in reincarnation perhaps more than we verbally admit, and our beliefs about it have multiple dimensions about (for example) whether our behavior in this life affects reincarnation in the next (karma) and whether our personalities and personal identities reappear in any future life. Only those who are atheists or (in many cases) agnostics as a group are solidly in the ranks of those with no belief in reincarnation in any form. Remember this point for now; I'll come back to it later in this chapter.

So if more of us believe in reincarnation than we realize in at least some form, is there any real evidence that supports those beliefs? Or are we just believing in the Tooth Fairy or the Great Pumpkin?

At the University of Virginia, researcher Ian Stevenson and his colleagues have spent decades tracking down reports of reincarnation from all over the world. A former department chairman in the psychiatry department at the university, he became interested in children who reported living previous lives. Eventually, he established the Division of Perceptual Studies at the university, which is probably the largest center for investigation of reincarnation in the United States. From the 1950s until his death in 2007, Stevenson rigorously investigated reports of reincarnation to determine their probable veracity and characteristics.

Jim Tucker is a child psychiatrist and one of Stevenson's colleagues at the University of Virginia. According to Tucker, the evidence for reincarnation varies according to the case, and, of course, no two cases are exactly alike. There are, however, some consistent types of information that are indicative of such cases. They have perhaps the most comprehensive collection of cases anywhere in the United States. Tucker wrote a highly readable account of some of the best evidence for reincarnation.[98]

One typical characteristic is that children make statements about their past lives almost as soon as they're old enough to talk. Generally these statements about their previous life nearly always start by the age of four, though occasionally it's delayed by as much as several years. Very often, young children make such statements, but as they grow older, the memories of the past life fades. Sometimes, however, the memories persist. The children do not try to impress anyone—they simply seem to be making ordinary comments about their (previous) daily life or comparing what happened in that life with what is happening to them currently. The children, if not the adults in their lives, tend to be quite matter-of-fact about their past lives.

Children also may be born with birthmarks or other physical markings that match markings or injuries from their previous life. In some cultures, it is the custom to specifically mark the body of a loved one with the hope that if the person is reincarnated the child may have matching marks and thus confirm the reincarnation.

Children are sometimes born after an "announcing dream" in which the mother or some other adult announces that the child will be born as a reincarnation of someone else. Most commonly the dreamer is the pregnant mother, but sometimes it is another female relative or close friend, or, occasionally, the father or other male relative who experiences the announcing dream. In some cultures the prediction of a reincarnation happens in the previous life—an elderly person may say he or she is coming back as a child to a particular friend or relative, for example.

Tucker also notes that children may start displaying behaviors or personality traits that correspond to their previous life but which are not displayed by family members in their current life. For example, one child in Sri Lanka showed a terror of trucks, even to the word "lorry" (the British English word for a truck) beginning as early as eight months old. As the child got a little older he made statements that tied him to a previous life in which he had been run down and killed by a truck. Sometimes this type of past-life recall emerges as odd types of playing. For example, one child in India consistently played at being a shop-keeper, which was eventually associated with a connection to a previous life as a shopkeeper. While many children may play such games, in this case it became almost obsessive.

Children may also recognize people, places, or objects from their past lives. This includes being able to name relatives and friends from the former life. Most famously, the identification of the current Dalai Lama when he was a small child was a result of the little boy's ability to recognize items from his previous life.

Most of the time, the past lives that children recall are recent ones (though there are some exceptions), and most often children recall only a single past life. In one of the studies at the University of Virginia, Stevenson cites the average time between death of the previous life and birth of the reincarnated child as only fourteen to sixteen months.[99] This is not a fixed duration, however. Jurgen Kiel has reported a case in Turkey of a little boy who recalled in great detail the life of a man who died fifty years before he was born.

Occasionally, in about 20 percent of the cases, children not only recall their past lives but also can talk about what their existence was like *between* lives. These reports include experiences like being taken by the hand by a "spirit being" and being led to a huge hall, where the child is told another life is waiting for him (or her). Sometimes they say they lingered in the area of their previous life or even attended (or viewed) their own funeral. In one case, a little girl in Thailand was upset because in her previous life, she had wanted her ashes buried under a favorite large tree at her local temple, and instead her family had scattered her ashes. Upon investigation, it turned out that the tree's root system made it too difficult to bury the ashes as requested, so the family had indeed scattered them.[100] In another case, a little boy reported "hovering" around the location where his body had been dumped. When he noticed his previous mother, his spirit followed her in an attempt to reunite with her but lost track of her when she went to a crowded market. Instead, however, he spotted the man who was to be his father in his current life, followed the man home, and decided to become part of his family. His current-life father confirmed that he had been at that market on that day.[101]

Frequently, the previous life is one that was cut short from the expected lifespan for that location and time. For example, Ian Stevenson discovered that in three separate cultures in Turkey, Ceylon, and Alaska, the age at death of the previous life was substantially younger than the expected lifespan for those locations.[102] For example, in his study, Turkish cases of reincarnation recalled previous lives that ended at a median age of thirty years, while the life expectancy was forty-eight years. In Ceylon, the previous lives ended at a median age of fourteen, while the life expectancy was sixty-one years; in Alaska, the median age at death for the previous lifetime was twenty-five years with a typical life expectancy of sixty-nine years. Thus, it may be true that previous lives are more likely to be recalled when the previous life was cut short.

Not all cases will include all these types of evidence, but this list provides the basic type of information that may be available. An example of a reincarnation case might illustrate a typical case. The one I'm presenting here was reported by Jurgen Keil from the University of Tasmania in Australia.[103] It concerns a girl born in a very remote village in Turkey and was investigated in two trips in 2008 and 2009 to the area in Turkey where she lived. At the time, the reincarnated child was fully adult at forty-six years old, but, atypically, still had a strong recollection of her previous life.

When the little girl, identified as M.C.,[104] was three years old, she spoke Turkish and Arabic with an odd accent and often cried and complained to her mother that "you're not my mother." She wanted to go visit her "real" mother and father who were "rich."[105] She mentioned names of friends and relatives of her previous life, but not her own name in that previous life.

M.C.'s parents were worried that the little girl would die if there was any contact with her previous life. They would also splash her face with water whenever she mentioned anything from her previous life in an attempt to get her to forget the previous life. Both are beliefs of this remote area of Turkey. Neither belief proved to be true for this little girl; the face-splashing didn't cause her to forget, and when she finally was allowed to contact her previous life family at the age of seventeen, she did not die.

M.C. at one stage mentioned that she had died in her previous life because she was shot while she attended a wedding. She also claimed that she had a married aunt in Izmir, and that she had lived in a house with oval windows.

When she was four years old (in this life), her father investigated and discovered the identity of her previous life by matching the names, the circumstances of death, and so on. In that previous life, she had been named P.P. All the names and other details M.C. had mentioned were proved true of the previous person's life. M.C. wanted to go visit her previous home, but her parents refused to take her and believed that (like many children who remember previous lives) she would eventually forget about it.

One day when she was about five years old, M.C. and her family were on the way to a town, and on the way, she pointed to a village visible from the road and said, "There is my village." It was indeed the village of P.P., located about five kilometers from M.C.'s home. (This is a substantial distance in this remote, mountainous area of Turkey, where travel is arduous at best and villages largely isolated.)

When M.C. was seventeen, her parents finally agreed to take her to P.P.'s village. Once they got to the edge of the village, M.C. was able to go directly to the house with the oval windows, but her former family no longer lived there, having moved away to a different village after P.P. had been shot and killed. Although her parents now lived elsewhere, they had returned to this village for a festival. M.C. spotted P.P.'s father and ran to him to the surprise and shock of everyone.[106]

There are more elements of this story, explained in more detail in the paper written by Keil. The point, however, is that virtually all the details M.C. remembered were correct about the little girl P.P. who had been shot and killed before M.C.'s birth.

In some ways, M.C.'s case is a little unusual because the memories of her former life never faded. It's more common for children to have the memories fade away after a few months or years.

Cases such as this one with M.C. are highly provocative. First, researchers verified the statements made by M.C. with numerous people, in the course of several interviews. Multiple interviews were conducted to determine if the details of the report changed over time, as well as interviews with multiple people to determine if different people gave different accounts. In the case of M.C., there was remarkable consistency across both time and individuals in terms of the details of the story.

It should also be remembered that this is not a singular case. Hundreds of cases much like this are in the University of

Virginia's archives, as well as reported by investigators in many other institutions.

As might be expected, given the current Western proclivity for materialism, reported cases of reincarnation are far more frequent in Asian societies than in the United States or western Europe. In part, this may be because parents in the United States are unresponsive toward children who begin talking about past lives. Those from a fundamentalist background (whether religious fundamentalism or from ardent atheism) may also believe such memories are either fantasies or the work of the devil and may deliberately suppress them. Nonetheless, such reports from the United States and western Europe do exist.

Consider, for example, the case of a New York City policeman named John, who was moonlighting as a security guard in 1992.[107] He discovered a robbery in progress and was shot six times. One bullet entered his back, went through his left lung, heart, and pulmonary artery. Though he was rushed to the emergency room, he was not able to survive such extensive wounds. John was a Roman Catholic, and reincarnation is not a tenet of that religion; nevertheless, John believed in reincarnation. At the time of his death, he had a daughter named Doreen to whom he was very close, and who he had promised to always take care of.

In 1997, Doreen gave birth to a little boy baby, whom she named William. Right after he was born, William had difficulty with fainting, and doctors diagnosed that he had pulmonary valve atresia, which happens when the pulmonary valve isn't properly formed. He also had a malformation of his right atrial chamber in his heart. Both those defects corresponded with the track of the bullet that killed his grandfather John. A coincidence, quite possibly. In any event, the problems were corrected with surgery and William is doing well.

Once William was old enough to talk, he started talking about his grandfather John's life—a grandfather who died five years before his birth. One day, when Doreen threatened to spank William if he continued to misbehave, he said, "Mom, when you were a little girl and I was your daddy, you were bad a lot of times, and I never hit you!"[108]

William also remembered details about his previous life from when Doreen was a little girl, correctly naming family pets from her childhood and noting which cat was the favorite of her father's.

Doreen once asked what William had experienced between the time he'd died as John and was born as William. William reported that he'd died on Thursday, had gone to heaven, and had the opportunity to talk with lots of animals. He then had the chance to talk to God, and he told God he was ready to return to Earth so he could be born on a Tuesday. At the time, William did not yet know the days of the week, so Doreen tested him by saying, "You died on a Tuesday and were born on a Thursday?" But William corrected her. John had indeed died on a Thursday, and William was born on a Tuesday.[109]

One item of interest is that none of these examples of reincarnation involve controversial recall techniques, such as hypnotism, past-life regression, or deep meditation. Don't get me wrong. I'm not saying that those techniques don't work, or that past lives recalled using them are incorrect. Heck, I've done my own bit of past-life meditations and discovered hundreds—even thousands—of such lives of my own.

The point is, however, that there may be alternative explanations for such experiences. For example, many complain that hypnosis places people in highly suggestible states where they may "create" memories of past lives. Another potential problem is that it may be that such past lives are actually accessing psychic memories from other people, rather than your own. For example, suppose you connect with the departed spirit of an individual, as was demonstrated chapter 7. If you then start reporting on a past life, it may be that you're tapping into that departed spirit rather than into your own past-life memories. It's not clear to me how reports generated in hypnotic and meditative states could be distinguished from a genuine reincarnation.

What distinguishes the reports noted above (and the hundreds of other reports in the University of Virginia archives) is that these reports were *not* generated in any type of altered state of consciousness. The children involved typically were extremely young, generally only two to four years old, when they began to report memories of previous lives. Their reports and memories were merely matter-of-fact statements. Many of the cases were very unwilling to report or receive any notoriety from their experiences. These reports typically include very specific and extensive details of those past lives—names, faces, pets, occupations, locations, details of both life, death, and funeral. Very often the previous life is one of someone unknown to the current family, often from another town. Despite this level of detail about lives that should be unknown, the specifics generally are carefully verified as true, confirmed by multiple witnesses, and validated by the investigators. Furthermore, virtually none of these reincarnation examples recall being anyone rich, famous, or historically important in significant ways. No Cleopatras, Henry VIIIs, or even Napoleons in this group!

Nonetheless, there is a scientific theory that just might account for actual reincarnation.

Ervin Laszlo is one of the great minds of our times. I had the privilege of interviewing him for my radio show when his book *Science and the Akashic Field: An Integral Theory of Everything* was released.[110] In addition to being a wonderful interview subject, he presented a fascinating new theory that attempts to understand all the phenomena that physics currently ignores (such as the psychic Black Swans discussed in this book). Laszlo insists that to be considered complete, it must be able to explain even these difficult-to-explain phenomena.[111]

Christopher Bache of the Department of Philosophy and Religious Studies at Youngstown State University reported an ongoing dialogue with Laszlo on the issue of reincarnation.[112] Laszlo presented his theory of the Akashic field (which he calls the A-field). This field is presumed to underlie the entire universe and provides the basis on which the universe is a single entity. Information about the universe is nonlocal; it is as if the universe itself is a single organism. In Laszlo's A-field, psychic phenomena are not bizarre, outrageous, or even unexpected. Laszlo brings the paranormal into the realm of the normal—and does it by *extending* current physics, not by destroying it.

Laszlo notes that the A-field accounts for many types of after-death communications (such as those reported in the Seventh Black Swan) as well as reincarnation experiences. This is because the A-field literally records *everything that ever happened everywhere in the universe.* In Lazlo's perspective, past-life memories and communications with the dead "have strong evidentiary support"[113] He notes, however, that some people find it easier to tap into that A-field to retrieve information that is not readily available to most. Laszlo claims that the A-field accumulates all learning in the universe and uses that learning to spawn new universes. This is also in agreement with the basic concepts of Rupert Sheldrake's morphogenetic fields.[114] In fact, the A-field may be a more developed form of the morphogenetic field that Sheldrake posited.

Reincarnation may be another variation on this A-field (or a subset of it) that Bache calls a soul field, which preserves the specifics of an individual—their learning and experiences. That soul field then grows with increasing incarnations, which improves the overall potential over many lives.[115]

Laszlo's interpretation is that it is less an individual's personality that is retained than that person's experiences and learning that goes into something like the collective unconscious of all of humanity. Bache's discussion of the details of both Laszlo's interpretation of reincarnation and his own perspective is well worth reading.

In essence, however, the message from these studies is that while current science may not know quite what to do with reports of reincarnation such as those presented in this chapter, it is not true there is no theory that encompasses such phenomena. In fact, another researcher, Amit Goswami, has a similar approach.

Amit Goswami is a theoretical nuclear physicist at the University of Oregon Institute for Theoretical Physics.[116] As such he has some serious chops with respect to science and our current understanding of the universe. He has been noted for pointing out the fundamental flaw of today's physics: Traditionally, science has placed matter and energy—the physical stuff of the universe—as the most important aspect of the universe. In Goswami's perspective, however, mystics are far more correct because mystics place *consciousness* at the center of the universe.[117] Goswami considers this "myopic" and believes that scientists must change their perspective away from matter and energy as primary and replace that by putting consciousness at the front and center of their studies. Goswami believes, with clear and careful justification, that doing so provides solid explanations for virtually all paranormal experiences as well as otherwise anomalous phenomena like reincarnation.

Reincarnation may or may not be part of your personal philosophy. Certainly my Methodist upbringing and intense training in the hard logic of physics left no room to even consider the possibility of reincarnation being a real phenomenon and not just fantasy or bogus experiences. Despite that rigid mindset, however, I have now changed my mind. The data collected clearly show that the statements by the reincarnated are far more than simple generalizations, imagination, and guesswork. The degree of specificity, details, and odd birth markings that correspond to previous-life wounds make it highly unlikely to be anything but the real thing.

So . . . given that Tinkerbell was born about thirteen months after my mother's death, and given the personality similarities between her and my mother, maybe it *is* the case that . . .

No. It *couldn't* be.

Could it?[118]

CHAPTER 9

A Bevy of Black Swans

As I mentioned in the introduction to this book, I started discovering my personal Black Swans when I began experiencing events I could not explain. These came about as a result of a "psychic awakening" after decades of being an absolute zero in terms of psychic abilities. In fact, I had never had the slightest psychic experience in my life until then. However, once I started exploring these areas, I realized that I can do virtually *all* psychic skills, though I'm not necessarily a star performer in them all.

My instinct tells me that if I can go from a "psychic zero" to "psychic," so can anyone else. In other words, my presumption is that there is nothing particularly special about me. If I can do it, I believe that so can pretty much anyone else. That's been my underlying assumption from the beginning.

Furthermore, my less-than-scientific directly observed evidence confirms that assumption. I've been giving workshops for years, and based on the feedback from those workshops, no matter how skeptical workshop participants may start out,[119] nearly everyone succeeds in at least one or two psychic skills. Usually it's spoon-bending—almost everyone is very successful at that. But every so often, a different skill is the one that unlocks the door to their psychic selves.

I once gave an advanced workshop for some folks who had taken my regular one a few months earlier. At the request of two of the participants, a mother-daughter pair, I reluctantly agreed to let the mother's husband—I'll call him Rich—participate in the workshop, even though he hadn't attended the first one. I asked them to come early so I could give him a little catch-up primer so he wouldn't be completely left behind in this more advanced workshop. This particular workshop was a two-day program, and for the entire first day, Rich amiably went along with all the exercises but had no real success with any of them. Even when he was able to bend his fork, he wasn't convinced. Over lunch break the first day he told me he was highly skeptical of anything psychic and had only agreed to attend because his wife and daughter had really wanted him to share in the workshop.

On the second day of the program, I had a remote-viewing exercise planned. I had carefully prepared a target and four possible comparison images. I had gone out of my way to ensure that, though I knew what the four possible images were, I had no clue what the actual target was. I gave the participants paper and pens, showed them the sealed target envelope, and gave them some simple directions on how to tune in to the target. I also encouraged them to draw the target and make simple notations about colors, textures, sounds, and smells.[120] Then I let them do their thing.

When everyone had finished, I went around the group, asking them to hold up their drawings and describe what they had perceived. Then I pulled out the four possible targets, one at a time, and asked them to judge their perceptions against each of the four drawings to determine which of the four was the closest match to what they had perceived.

Interestingly, in this small group of about eight people, five of them keyed in on one of the four judging images with varying degrees of clarity. This image showed several stacks of coins against a white background. Two other participants had only vague hits that didn't match any of the drawings very well. Rich, however, drew a nearly exact match of another possible drawing, a curving country road. He got the layout of the picture perfectly—almost to the degree that if you put his drawing over the judging image, it looked as if he could have traced it. It was that exact.

However, since so many people had cued in on the stacks of coins, we all expected the actual target envelope to reveal that image. And when I opened it, the image revealed was . . . the curving country road! Rich had totally *nailed* the remote-viewing exercise. For the first time that weekend, he felt as if he were a star in that exercise—and he was!

I could sympathize with Rich's astonishment, because my own remote-viewing success the first time I tried blew me away, too. Rich will probably never be a particularly good psychic medium or a healer or any other type of psychic, but he could well have a real talent for remote viewing. I hope he practiced that skill to develop his talent.

That is what I have observed about psychic skills over the past decade or more. They are very similar to other human talents in that everyone seems to be able to do them at least sometimes and under some circumstances, just as pretty much everyone can learn to plunk out "Chopsticks" on a piano—even me! Yet such occasional hits do not necessarily mean they're an especially talented psychic. Just as a musician needs to learn how to play his instrument, and then work hard to practice-practice-practice, psychic skills need the same determination and hard work to lift above the mediocre to the exceptional. It also helps to realize that no one is equally talented in all psychic skills. A great remote viewer may well be a terrible healer and an even worse medium. An excellent medium may be a horrible remote viewer and only so-so at spoon-bending.

The point is that psychic talents should be considered on the same spectrum as all other human talents, with people having varying degrees of natural ability in particular skills, and yet still requiring work and practice to learn how to use those skills to the best of their abilities.

My bevy of Black Swans, both those personally experienced and those observed in workshop participants, have more than convinced me of the reality of psychic skills. Because I do recognize that my personal experiences are convincing only to me, I also have reviewed the scientific evidence of these skills in the earlier chapters. Let's review that evidence for the various skills discussed here.

The First Black Swan: Psychokinesis

The fine art of spoon-bending (or metal-bending) shows every indication of being a nearly universal human capability. In my workshops, I've taught hundreds and hundreds of people to do it. The thing about bending a spoon (or fork) is that if you've done it yourself, you know that it's not a fake. If you watch someone else do it, there's always a question in your mind over whether it's a trick or reality. This is why I ruin a lot of good-quality forks in my workshops. The reason isn't to show people how to do a party trick. The real reason is to *unequivocally prove to them* that they have the psychic skill to do it themselves, at least under certain circumstances. A warped fork or spoon cannot be imagined away. I encourage people to take their cutlery home with them so they leave with that tangible *proof* of their ability to do the "impossible."[121] I do ask people to bend responsibly once they know how to do it, of course!

Furthermore, as I pointed out, it has been known for thirty years that the crystalline structure of psychically bent spoons and forks has very different characteristics than the structure of mechanically deformed cutlery. In other words, *it is possible to determine through objective laboratory tests which warped forks were psychically bent and which were mechanically deformed.* While not everyone carries appropriate laboratory microscopes around in their pockets, it is possible to have psychically bent examples tested for confirmation. Frauds and stage magicians mechanically deform their spoons; psychics bend them an entirely different way—with their minds.

The Second Black Swan: Remote Viewing

If ever there is a psychic skill that has been studied upside down and sideways, it is remote viewing. In spite of the claims of the debunkers, there are people who are incredibly talented remote viewers and who can produce astonishing and highly detailed drawings of places and objects far beyond their five physical senses. Any thoughtful, open-minded contemplation of the data collected on remote viewing has to acknowledge that there clearly are cases where highly significant successes have been achieved.

Not everyone is a wonderful remote viewer. About 1 percent of the population seems to have the potential to be terrific at it—that natural talent thing again. But almost everyone seems to be able to do it under at least some circumstances. The evidence, once again, is quite strong. Even notorious skeptic Ray Hyman had to admit not only that the evidence was extremely strong, but also that he could not find any flaw in the experimental protocols used by the military programs. Still, he concluded without any firm basis that the remote viewing *must* have flaws because otherwise they'd mean psychic skills are real, and he simply didn't believe that could be true.

Such closed-minded, far-from-objective reviews of the data are fairly typical of those who try to debunk psychic skills.

The Third Black Swan: Energy Healing

I have to admit that until my own personal experience of being healed psychically by my extraordinarily talented friend Deb, I had viewed energy healing with a heavy dose of skepticism. I frankly attributed stories of healings to something on the order of the placebo effect in which people receiving healing simply convince themselves that they're better. However, after the experiences I had, I have had to change my mind about this psychic skill, too. Clearly, something other than imagination is at work.

Also provocative was the evidence for the effectiveness of prayer in helping animals heal from self-inflicted wounds. The bush babies in this study were stressed, and that stress led them to scratch at themselves in their grooming sessions, opening up nasty wounds. This very well-designed controlled study demonstrated that the prayed-for group of bush babies showed significant improvements in their healing, reduced stress, and improved behaviors when compared to the group that was not prayed for. By studying nonhuman subjects, the potential of confusion that could result from prayer generated by family and friends was eliminated.

Healing is one of the best-studied psychic effects. Clearly, significant data supporting its efficacy exist in the scientific record. While the limits and mode of efficacy of psychic healing isn't well understood, it does seem clear that it works.

The Fourth Black Swan: Telepathy

Telepathy experiments are notoriously tricky to do well. It's hard to separate out the specifics of whether a successful outcome is the result of telepathy or something else. Sheldrake's email study, however, showed very clearly that to a degree significantly above random chance, people *do* know who has sent them messages before they receive them. Just as I regularly call my friend Caro just as she's about to hit "send" in her email program, we know when friends and family are thinking about us.

Still, as I pointed out, it can be hard to determine if the result is due to telepathy or due to some other psychic skill such as remote viewing or other clairsentience capability. Perhaps the specifics don't matter all that much. What does matter is that there is some solid, scientific evidence that we sometimes do know information that comes from beyond our five physical senses.

The Fifth Black Swan: Animal Telepathy

I am very attached to my pets, as many people are. For the past couple of decades, my pets have been cats; before that I always had dogs. I am very aware of the ability of my pets to understand my moods, the meaning behind a high percentage of my words—at least in terms of emotional content if not always specifics—and their ability to respond to my needs. As with the telepathy, however, there are also solid scientific data that support animals' abilities to know the intentions of their owners to return home at the time they make such decisions, irrespective of location of the owner, the length of the time it will take the owner to actually arrive home, and the impossibility of the animal to get direct sensory information about that decision. Professional skeptics have tried to pick holes in Sheldrake's study to no avail—and in fact, they themselves have been shown to have made a number of fraudulent statements, not to mention flat-out lies in their attempts to negate Sheldrake's work.

The challenge in proving animal telepathy is that we always have to infer what the animal knows by their external behaviors. Sheldrake's clever study of dogs (and cats, horses, parrots, cockatiels, snakes, cows, sheep, owls, mynahs, and miscellaneous other animals) that know when their owners are coming home used a clever protocol that provided clear evidence that the animals know *something* about their owners' decisions at the time they make them.[122] While the data for dogs is clear, the anecdotal evidence supporting other animals is sufficiently similar to that of dogs that there seems little reason to deny that the ability is general to animals with strong emotional bonds with their owners.

What isn't clear is whether animals that haven't shown such behavior (i.e., rabbits, rats, gerbils, hamsters, guinea pigs, and fish) do not demonstrate the behavior because they are incapable of knowing that information, because they do not associate their owners' return with a happy reunion, or because they simply don't have a strong emotional bond to their owners.

The Sixth Black Swan: Precognition

If I had guessed, fifteen years ago, whether there was any evidence that supported the ability of humans to perceive the future, I would have laughed myself silly. The whole concept of looking into the future would have seemed ridiculous—of *course* we can't do that! It's against the laws of physics, right?

Wrong. The evidence in favor of precognition is stunning. We now know that we react to emotionally charged events on an unconscious level at least two seconds before they happen—and that we know what type of emotionally charged event will occur (i.e., whether the event is arousing or fear-producing). Happily for all of physics, our new understanding of quantum mechanics, and new interpretations of the equations that define quantum mechanics offer a way of accepting that time isn't exactly the straight-line, single-branched river we have thought it was. Whether these new interpretations are sufficient to explain our ability to look into the future, or whether quantum mechanics will have to be superseded by a more expansive theory, sooner or later science is going to have to deal with the reality that we can look into the future.

The Seventh Black Swan: Survival after Death

If you thought precognition was a huge no-no in science, just try getting funding to investigate the possibility that some part of us survives physical death. The University of Arizona has been a leader in this field (though possibly to the extreme discomfort of some of the faculty not involved in the research conducted there). Starting with Gary Schwartz's series of carefully designed and ever-more stringent studies of professional mediums, and moving beyond that to more recent studies by others coming out of that program, the data clearly show that at least some talented mediums are able to achieve accuracy records that are several times better than control groups achieve. With many experiments attaining results in the 85 to 95 percent accuracy level, it is very hard to explain how the data can be caused solely by chance.

Survival after death is a concept that virtually *all* human societies have assumed as a truth, possibly going back as far as the Neanderthals, who demonstrated clear signs of ritual burial of some group members. Included with those burials was evidence of flowers laid over the deceased, along with useful and probably highly valued grave goods buried (presumably) for use by the deceased in the afterlife. It is, in fact, *only* our secular Western society that even questions whether some part of us survives death. Does that make us smarter than other societies? Or does it make us more blind?

Given the scientific data now being generated in careful, well-designed studies, it is hard to justify clinging to a belief that doesn't agree with the scientific evidence. But those who insist that there is no survival after death are doing exactly that.

The Eighth Black Swan: Reincarnation

If the data exists that we survive physical death, is it possible that we might come back and live a new life in some form? As it happens, although Western religions do not necessarily embrace the concept of reincarnation, other religions do. Western science tends to lump "religion" in the context of the big three—Christianity, Judaism, and Islam—with the result that highly ethnocentric assumptions are made about what "religion" believes.

The point is that the degree of evidence for reincarnation is difficult to dismiss—and cases exist not only in reincarnation-friendly cultures, but also in Western society, though we tend to call such cases delusional. This evidence, though often derided as "anecdotal," consists of far more than generalized statements. The cases investigated include place names, personal names, descriptions of personality characteristics and habits associated with individuals by name, identification of specific items owned by or associated with specific individuals—including being able to choose them from a random assortment of other similar items—birthmarks or other physical and emotional traumas associated with past lives or the cause of death of a previous life, knowledge of locations where previous lives were lived, despite never having been there before, recognition of places and people from the previous life, and so on.

A recent television "documentary" showed a skeptic trying to point out that a half-dozen statements made about a previous life were simply made up fantasies. He gave a volunteer the opportunity to fantasize about what kind of life the volunteer might have lived previously (despite that the volunteer had no such memory). There were perhaps half a dozen different questions about gender, time period, profession, cause of death, and so on. The skeptic noted that the answers to those very specific questions agreed with one of his previously prepared sets of possible combinations quite nicely. From this the skeptic concluded that stories of reincarnation are mere happenstance.

The fact is that such "proofs" are themselves parlor tricks because they *do not speak to the evidence that exists.* The reincarnation stories studied at the University of Virginia and by other researchers worldwide are not a half-dozen statements of very general questions. The cases investigated are complex, detailed, memories of complete lives, including highly specific names, places, dates, events, objects, people, animals, and so on. These cases have dozens of highly detailed facts in them, not just a handful of generalizations. And those facts have been verified.

Reincarnation does not lend itself to standard double-blind controlled studies, which means that it's challenging to get reincarnation studies taken seriously by scientists. That said, if you read through the accounts of reincarnation collected in the archives at the University of Virginia and reported by the researchers there, it's very difficult to disbelieve the reality of these accounts. The evidence for reincarnation is actually quite strong, even if the data are the result of interviews rather than double-blind experiments.

These eight Black Swans are some of the key signposts that have convinced me of the reality of psychic effects. My personal experiences in each of these, combined with the scientific data that supports each of them, have combined to make me a believer. Bear in mind that fifteen or twenty years ago I had the exact opposite opinion about psychic talents. But the data are highly convincing—*if* you're willing to look at the data with an open mind.

Of course, it also helps if you've had the inexplicable, confounding experiences I've had. While one such experience can be dismissed, the sheer number and frequency of confounding experiences are also highly convincing.

So what conclusions can be drawn in general about these psychic experiences? I think there are some general points that can be made.

- The most important conclusion is that these psychic phenomena are *real* phenomena. We may not know how to explain them at the moment, but shouldn't that be a call to demand that we investigate them and figure out why and how they happen instead of sweeping them under the rug and ignoring them?

- Psychic phenomena are not constrained by physical distance. Remote viewing, telepathy, animal telepathy, have all been demonstrated to operate at long distances with no additional effort than if the information is next door.

- Psychic phenomena are also not constrained by time. It is as easy to remote view the past and future as it is the present, for example, and there is plenty of evidence that unconsciously we anticipate events before they happen and can exhibit other precognitive skills.

- Psychic phenomena are not limited by physical barriers, walls, oceans, underground burials, electromagnetic shielding, or other physical barriers. None of those stop remote viewers.

- Psychic skills are not solely the domain of human beings. It is very clear that a broad array of animals have psychic skills too. To ignore that is to throw away important data.

These general points are the exact issues that are difficult for science to accept because they seem to run counter to current understanding of how the universe works. Yet that "understanding" is really constrained by classical physics, not current knowledge of quantum mechanics as it underlies our macroscopic world. When compared to quantum mechanical reality, psychic phenomena aren't nearly so outrageous as they are when compared to classical physics. And when cutting edge theories such as those by respected researchers like Ervin Laszlo or Amit Goswami, psychic phenomena move very clearly from the "paranormal" to the "normal."

And that is the real mandate that comes out of this review of the evidence. It's time that science stops viewing psychic phenomena as bizarre, outrageous, and inappropriate for scientific study. We can never have a comprehensive, complete understanding of the universe until we have a theory that not only includes classical mechanics and quantum mechanics, but *also* includes well documented psychic phenomena. The scientific data that support the existence of these phenomena are real. They're solid. They're generated using well thought out, carefully designed studies. It's about time that science and scientists stop attacking the personal reputation of researchers who generate these data, and start trying to formulate theories that explain them in the context of solid scientific concepts.

Borrowing tricks from stage magicians, the skeptics attempt to "disprove" reincarnation and other psychic phenomena using mere sleight-of-hand.[123] They do not address the data in any way. While they're amusing you with a clever trick, they hope you don't notice that they're busy burying and ignoring the actual data and research protocols used by the researchers. Frankly, it's long past time for such nonsense to stop. It's unprofessional, insulting, and borderline libelous to continue such attacks. Not to mention that it's totally unscientific.

Don't get me wrong. I'm not saying that all psychic research is perfect. Nor am I insisting that it cannot be subjected to scientific scrutiny. My objections arise when the level of scrutiny psychic researchers are subjected to far exceeds that of any other researchers in any other discipline. I once heard a physicist say that the data in support of the Big Bang theory is orders of magnitude less robust than the data in support of any psychic phenomenon—and yet, most scientists accept some version of the Big Bang as fact, while adamantly rejecting psychic events as imaginary, hoaxes, or pure fictions.

Any time you're trying to measure a human behavior or talent, whether it's healing a sick person, telepathic communication, or surviving death, you're going to run into difficulties in designing a replicable study protocol. Many of these types of events, such as reincarnation, are not repeatable. On the other hand, Schwartz's brilliant protocols with mediums in studying access to previously departed spirits demonstrates that solid science *can* be done, even with such difficult topics.

What I do say is that the professional skeptic needs to stop being a stage performer and start actually looking seriously at the data and the protocols presented to them. They have to stop throwing the data away simply because they don't like it. They have to start demonstrating an open, scientific mind and begin to pay attention to some fascinating and poorly understood events that offer some major clues that our understanding of the universe is still incomplete.

Of course, some of the most commonly seen debunkers simply have few or no scientific credentials at all. They have built their entire careers around dismissing the reality of what clearly happens. For this type of "expert," there is no way they can afford to admit that they've been lying through their teeth for decades because their personal and professional reputations would be in tatters—not to mention that their ego-gratifying sources of income and public acclaim would be equally shattered. Instead, it is important for the media to understand that these people, quite simply, do not know what they're talking about. They don't understand the subjects they're dismissing, they don't even bother to look at the evidence, and they clearly have not the slightest clue about what the scientific process actually means.

Breakthroughs in science happen when researchers have the courage to set aside "accepted wisdom" and take seriously the results of experiments that seem to contradict such "known truth." A couple of examples may illustrate what I mean.

The Michelson-Morley experiment in 1887 attempted to measure properties of the "ether" that accepted wisdom assured them pervaded the universe[124]—and the researchers couldn't find a single trace of that "luminiferous" ether.[125] Rather than ignoring their results and throwing their data away by assuming that the *experiment* might be fraudulent (as today's skeptics would have us do with psychic experimental data), the Michelson-Morley experiment was explained by FitzGerald and Lorentz in terms of a length contraction of space itself—and that, in turn, was used by Einstein in generating his theory of special relativity in 1905.

Yet for nearly twenty years, no real understanding of the Michelson-Morley data existed—*the data came* before *the theory.* The data, in fact, provided the foundation that the theory rested upon. Once Einstein's theory of special relativity was formed, then later experiments were designed to test it. But the initial data—the data that measured the anomalous events that had to somehow be explained—that data came first.

In 1909, Ernest Rutherford directed Hans Geiger and Ernest Marsden in an investigation of the structure of the atom. At the time, the current "accepted wisdom" was that the atom had a structure similar to a plum pudding in which the small negative electrons floated in a positively charged "batter."[126] The Geiger-Marsden experiment consisted of shooting a beam of positively charged particles at a thin foil of gold.[127] The idea was that Thomson's model predicted that such a beam would be mildly deflected from its path because the positive particles in the beam would be repelled as it passed through the (mostly) positively charged "batter" of the atoms in the foil. By looking at the angles of deflection, Geiger and Marsden hoped to get more details about the inner structure of the atom.

That they did, in fact. Unfortunately, the details they discovered had nothing to do with plum puddings. Instead of the minor deflections expected, the vast majority of the positive particle beam went straight through the foil with no deflection at all. A few of the particles, however, were deflected—but not mildly. Instead, they bounced back at very sharp angles, some even bouncing backward! As Rutherford later noted:

> *It was quite the most incredible event that has ever happened to me in my life. It was almost as incredible as if you fired a fifteen-inch shell at a piece of tissue paper and it came back and hit you.*[128]

This data could have been thrown out as anomalous, rejected because it was so weird and extreme, or ignored because it didn't fit the researchers' expectations—just as mainstream science and much of the media treats experimental results from scientific psychic research today. Instead, Rutherford thought long and hard about what the data might mean. His result was a new model of the atom, the Rutherford model, built on the presumption that data from careful experiments mattered more than the current sacred cows of accepted beliefs.

I could go on and on. The important breakthroughs in science come *not* from data that reinforce existing theories, as important as that data may be. The real breakthroughs—the ones that generate innovations and leaps forward in science—come when someone does an experiment and produces data that *conflict* with our existing understanding of the world. When that data is considered carefully, it leads to new models and new understanding. It expands our knowledge of the universe.

Looking at anomalous results from well-conceived experiments is not outside the realm of science, as some would have you believe. Looking at those results *is* science. It's what science is supposed to be all about: Finding explanations for phenomena that clearly exist but that we don't now understand.

Carl Sagan's (in)famous assertion that "extraordinary claims require extraordinary evidence" needs to be pitched into the trash heap, which is where it has belonged from the beginning. Ignoring data you don't like or can't explain is the *opposite* of scientific. The corrected version needs to be "extraordinary claims require extraordinary *investigation*."

In other words, Science, you've got a lot of work to do.

Little Brunhilda found her Black Swan. In fact, she found a whole bevy of them. She was thinking of setting up a Black Swan sanctuary and charging admission to those who wanted to experience Black Swans for themselves. Happily for the rest of the populace of the kingdom, that wasn't necessary because the philosopher-king decreed that Black Swans were the new royal mascot and moved a family of them into the public park outside his palace where everyone could see them and prove for themselves that Black Swans are very real indeed.

And Brunhilda, happy to have toppled the orthodoxy in the kingdom, also toppled the philosopher-king, took over his seat as the head of the Truth Committee, and she spent her life puncturing egos and dogmas wherever she found them to excess.

And she lived happily ever after.

The End.

Reading List

This reading list is organized, first by papers and sources used in researching the various Black Swan chapters in this book. In the course of that research I came across a number of other interesting papers on subjects that did not make it into this book for various reasons. Because I believe these research studies may also be of interest to readers, I have included them as "Other Topics" and organized them into subtopics also.

I am aware that few people have easy access to the academic libraries where the research papers are available. With that in mind, I offer a separate list of Recommended Books. These tend to be highly readable volumes that are packed with information about subjects of interest to readers of this book. I have all these volumes on my personal bookshelf and can recommend them highly.

The Black Swans

Chapter 1: Psychokinesis

Bosch, H.; Steinkamp, F.; Biller, E. (2006). Examining Psychokinesis: The Interaction of Human Intention with Random Number Generators—A Meta-Analysis. *Psychological Bulletin*, 132 (4), 497–523.

Dagnall, N.; Parker, A.; Munley, G.; Drinkwater, K. (2010). Common Paranormal Belief Dimensions. *Journal of Scientific Exploration*, 24 (3), 477–94.

Hasted, J.; Robertson, D. (1979). The Details of Paranormal Metal-Bending. *Journal of the Society for Psychical Research,* 50 (77), 9–20.

Helfrich, W. (2011). Are There Stable Mean Values, and Relationships between Them, in Statistical Parapsychology? *Journal of Scientific Exploration,* 25 (1), 7–28.

Kugel, W. (2011). A Faulty PK Meta-Analysis. *Journal of Scientific Exploration.* 25 (1), 47–62.

Moddel, G. (2006). Entropy and Information Transmission in Causation and Retrocausation. *AIP Conference Proceedings,* 863 (1), 62–74.

Morse, D. R. (2010). The Evidence for Psychokinesis. *Journal of Spirituality & Paranormal Studies,* 33 (1), 1–3.

Radin, D. (1997). *The Conscious Universe: The Scientific Truth of Psychic Phenomena.* San Francisco, CA: HarperEdge. See particularly chapter 8, Mind-Matter Interaction, 127–46.

Radin, D.; Nelson, R.; Dobyns, Y.; Houtkooper, J. (2006). Reexamining Psychokinesis: Comment on Bosch, Steinkamp, and Boller (2006). *Psychological Bulletin,* 132 (4), 529–32.

Rietdijk, C. W. (2007). Four-Dimensional Physics, Nonlocal Coherence, and Paranormal Phenomena. *Physics Essays,* 20 (2), 169–96.

Severin, D. (1985). Remote Annealing of High Carbon Steel Parts, *ARCHAEUS,* 3 (Summer 1985).

Shen, D. (2010). Unexpected Behavior of Matter in Conjunction with Human Consciousness. *Journal of Scientific Exploration.* 24 (1), 41–52.

Smith, P. H. (2005). *Reading the Enemy's Mind: Inside Star Gate— America's Psychic Espionage Program.* New York, NY: Forge Press.

Chapter 2: Remote Viewing

Abramson, P. R. (1997). Probing Well Beyond the Bounds of Conventional Wisdom. *American Journal of Political Science,* 41 (2), 675–82.

Bradley, R. T. (2007). The Psychophysiology of Intuition: A Quantum-Holographic Theory of Nonlocal Communication. *World Futures: The Journal of General Evolution*, 63 (2), 61–97.

Buchanan, L. (2003). *The Seventh Sense: The Secrets of Remote Viewing as told by a "Psychic Spy" for the U.S. Military.* New York, NY: Paraview Pocket Books.

Druckman, D.; Swets, J. A. (Editors). (1988). *Enhancing Human Performance: Issues, Theories, and Techniques.* Washington, DC: National Academy Press.

Graham, D. (2006). Experimental Data Demonstrating Augmentation of Ambient Gravitational and Geomagnetic Fields. *AIP Conference Proceedings* 813 (1) 1256–63.

Haraldsson, E.; Gerding, J. L. F. (2010). Fire in Copenhagen and Stockholm: Indridason's and Swedenborg's "Remote Viewing" Experiences. *Journal of Scientific Explorations*, 24 (3), 425–36.

Howard, R. G. (2010). Can an Ordinary Person Be Trained to Use the Psychic Senses? *Journal of Spirituality & Paranormal Studies*, 33 (2), 101–10.

Hyman, R. (1996). Evaluation of a Program on Anomalous Mental Phenomena. *Journal of Scientific Exploration*, 10 (1), 31–58.

Lora, D. (2003). "How I Was a Psychic Spy for the CIA and Found God." *Noetic Sciences Review,* Sep–Nov 2003 (65), 32–35.

Mack, J.; Powell, L. (2005). Perceptions of Non-Local Communication: Incidences Associated with Media Consumption and Individual Differences. *North American Journal of Psychology*, 7 (2), 279–94.

May, E. C. (1996). The American Institutes for Research Review of The Department of Defense's STAR GATE Program: A Commentary. *Journal of Scientific Exploration*, 10 (1), 89–108.

May, E. C.; Lantz, N. D. (2010). Anomalous Cognition Technical Trials: Inspiration for the Target Entropy Concept. *Journal of the Society for Psychical Research*, 74 (901), 225–43.

McGrath-Whitman, N. (2003). Peril in Terrorist Work. *Journal of Religion & Psychical Research*, 26 (3), 152–57.

McMoneagle, J. (1997). *Mind Trek: Exploring Consciousness, Time, and Space Through Remote Viewing.* Charlottesville, VA: Hampton Roads Publishing.

McMoneagle, J. (1998). *The Ultimate Time Machine: A Remote Viewer's Perception of Time, and Predictions for the New Millennium.* Charlottesville, VA: Hampton Roads Publishing.

McMoneagle, J. (2000). *Remote Viewing Secrets: A Handbook.* Charlottesville, VA: Hampton Roads Publishing.

McMoneagle, J. (2002). *The Stargate Chronicles: Memoirs of a Psychic Spy.* Charlottesville, VA: Hampton Roads Publishing.

Perez-Navarro, J. M.; Lawrence, T.; Hume, I. (2009). Personality, Mental State and Procedure in the Experimental Replication of ESP: A Preliminary Study of New Variables. *Journal of the Society for Psychical Research*, 73 (894), 17–32.

Puthoff, H. E. (1996). The CIA & ESP: Taking the Wraps Off Government Remote Viewing Experiments. *Noetic Sciences Review*, Summer 1996, (38), 19–22.

Puthoff, H. E. (1996a). CIA-Initiated Remote Viewing Program at Stanford Research Institute. *Journal of Scientific Exploration*, 10 (1), 63–76.

Smith, P. H. (2005). *Reading the Enemy's Mind: Inside Star Gate—America's Psychic Espionage Program.* New York, NY: Forge Press.

Stanescu, A. (2010). The Role of Telepathy and Clairvoyance in Criminology. *Proceedings of the 4th World Conference on the Advancement of Scholarly Research in Science, Economics, Law & Culture*, 2010, 259–63.

Swann, I. (1996). *Remote Viewing: The Real Story, An Autobiographical Memoir.* Web ebook, partial manuscript available at *http://www.biomindsuperpowers.com/Pages/2.html.*

Targ, R. (1996). Remarkable Distant Viewing. *Noetic Sciences Review*, Summer 1996 (38), 22–23.

Targ, R. (1996a). Remote Viewing at Stanford Research Institute in the 1970s: A Memoir. *Journal of Scientific Exploration*, 10 (1), 77–88.

Utts, J. (1996). An Assessment of the Evidence for Psychic Functioning. *Journal of Scientific Exploration*, 10 (1), 3–30.

Utts, J. (1996a). Response to Hyman. *Journal of Scientific Exploration*, 10 (1), 59–62.

Weintraub, P. (2005). Eyes Only: The Real X-Files. *Psychology Today*, 38 (6), 78.

Chapter 3: Healing

Agdal, R. (2005). Diverse and Changing Perceptions of the Body: Communicating Illness, Health, and Risk in an Age of Medical Pluralism. *The Journal of Alternative & Complementary Medicine*, 11 (Supplement 1 2005), S67–S75.

Andrade, C.; Radhakrishnan, R. (2009). Prayer and Healing: A Medical and Scientific Perspective on Randomized Controlled Trials. *Indian Journal of Psychiatry*, 51 (4), 247–53.

Bonapartian, E. (2006). Applying Reiki to Our Dreams. *Reiki News Magazine*, Fall 2006, 39–43.

Breslin, M. J.; Lewis, C. A. (2008). Theoretical Models of the Nature of Prayer and Health: A Review. *Mental Health, Religion & Culture*, 11 (1), 9–21.

Brown, M. H. (2001). A Psychosynthesis Twelve Step Program for Transforming Consciousness: Creative Explorations of . . . *Counseling & Values*, 45(2), 103.

Cadge, W. (2009). Saying Your Prayers, Constructing Your Religions: Medical Studies of Intercessory Prayer. *Journal of Religion*, 89 (3), 299–327.

DiNucci, E. M. (2005). Energy Healing: A Complementary Technique for Orthopaedic and Other Conditions. *Orthopaedic Nursing*, 24 (4), 259–69.

Dossey, L. (1999). Dreams and Healing: Reclaiming a Lost Tradition. *Alternative Therapies in Health & Medicine*, 5 (6), 12–17.

Epstein, D. M.; Senzon, S. A.; Lemberger, D. (2009). Reorganizational Healing: A Paradigm for the Advancement of Wellness, Behavior Change, Holistic Practice, and Healing. *The Journal of Alternative & Complementary Medicine*, 15 (5), 475–87.

Ernst, L. S. (2004). Polarity Addresses the "Whole" in Holistic. *Holistic Nursing Practice*, March/April 2004, 63–66.

Eschiti, V. S. (2007). Healing Touch: A Low-Tech Intervention in High-Tech Settings. *Dimensions of Critical Care Nursing*, 26 (1), 9–14.

Franklin, E. F. (2007). Sound Therapy. *Massage Magazine*, April 2007, 86–93.

Franklin, E. F.; Jackson, K. (2008). Energetic Ethics. *Massage Magazine*, June 2008, 22–24.

Gerber, R. (2000). *A Practical Guide to Vibrational Medicine: Energy Healing and Spiritual Transformation*. New York, NY: HarperCollins Publishers.

Gordon, R. (2002). *Quantum Touch: The Power to Heal*. Berkeley, CA: North Atlantic Books.

Harman, R. (2011). Is It Time to Integrate Medical and Natural Health Care? *Kai Tiaki Nursing New Zealand*, 17 (1), 26–27.

Harrison, K. K. (2003). Reiki Aura Clearing and Psychotherapy. *Reiki News Magazine*, Summer 2003, 23–26. Available online at *http://www.spiritualone.com/Online/July03/JulyNL03.htm*.

Jackson, E.; Kelley, M.; McNeil, P.; Meyer, E.; Schlegel, L.; Eaton, M. (2008). Does Therapeutic Touch Help Reduce Pain and Anxiety in Patients with Cancer? *Clinical Journal of Oncology Nursing*, 12 (1), 113–20.

Jain, S.; Mills, P. (2010). Biofield Therapies: Helpful or Full of Hype? A Best Evidence Synthesis. *International Journal of Behavioral Medicine*, 2010 (17), 1–16.

Johnson, B. (1999). Holistic nursing: A breed of its own. *Tennessee Nurse*, 62 (1), 11.

Johnston, L.; Boxtel, A. (2010). Stem-Cell Consciousness: The Divine Ground of Healing. *The Townsend Letter*, June 2010, 50–55.

Jonas, W. B.; Crawford, C. C. (2004). The Healing Presence: Can It Be Reliably Measured? *The Journal of Alternative & Complementary Medicine*, 10 (5), 751–56.

Lazar, S. G. (2001). Knowing, Influencing, and Healing: Paranormal Phenomena and Implications for Psychoanalysis and Psychotherapy. *Psychoanalytic Inquiry*, 21 (1), 113–31.

Lesniak, K. T. (2006). The Effect of Intercessory Prayer on Wound Healing in Nonhuman Primates. *Alternative Therapies in Health & Medicine*, 12 (6), 42–48.

Liebert, M. A. (2004). Report on the First Annual Research Symposium on Energetic and Spiritual Processes of Healing. *The Journal of Alternative & Complementary Medicine*, 10 (4), 715–17.

MacIntyre, B.; Hamilton, J.; Fricke, T.; Ma, W.; Mehle, S.; Michel, M. (2008). The Efficacy of Healing Touch in Coronary Artery Bypass Surgery Recovery: A Randomized Clinical Trial. *Alternative Therapies*, 14 (4), 24–32.

Means. L. G. (2010). Healing Rhythms: Music and Vibration Augment Massage. *Massage Magazine*, February 2010, 68–73.

Moga, M. M.; Bengston, W. F. (2010). Anomalous Magnetic Field Activity During a Bioenergy Healing Experiment. *Journal of Scientific Exploration*, 24 (3), 397–410.

Narayanasamy, A.; Narayanasamy, M. (2008). The Healing Power of Prayer and Its Implications for Nursing. *British Journal of Nursing*, 17 (6), 394–98.

Radin, D.; Lobach, E. (2007). Toward Understanding the Placebo Effect: Investigating a Possible Retrocausal Factor. *The Journal of Alternative & Complementary Medicine*, 13 (7), 733–40.

Radin, D.; Taft, R.; Yount, G. (2004). Effects of Healing Intention on Cultured Cells and Truly Random Events. *Journal of Alternative & Complementary Medicine*, 10 (1), 103–112.

Robb, W. J. W. (2006). Self-Healing: A Concept Analysis. *Nursing Forum*, 41 (2), 60–76.

Rosenbaum, R. (2011). Exploring the Other Dark Continent: Parallels between Psi Phenomena and the Psychotherapeutic Process. *Psychoanalytic Review*, 98 (1), 57–90.

Schlitz, M.; Radin, D.; Malle, B. F.; Schmidt, S.; Utts, J.; Yount, G. L. (2003). Distant Healing Intention: Definitions and Evolving Guidelines for Laboratory Studies. *Alternative Therapies in*

Health & Medicine, 9 (3): Definitions and Standards in Healing Research: A31–A43.

Schuldt, H. (2002). Bio-energetic Medicine Is Sufficiently Mature to Be Incorporated into Standard Medical Practice. *Townsend Letter for Doctors and Patients,* July 2002, 78–81.

Shore, A. G. (2004). Long-Term Effects of Energetic Healing on Symptoms of Psychological Depression and Self-Perceived Stress. *Alternative Therapies,* 10 (3), 42–48.

Smith, K. (2006). Bioenergetics: A New Science of Healing. *Shift: At the Frontiers of Consciousness,* March–May 2006 (10), 11–13, 34.

Targ, E. (1999). Distant Healing. *Noetic Sciences Review,* (49), 24.

VanderVaart, S.; Gijsen, V. M. G. J.; de Wildt, S. N.; Koren, G. (2009). A Systematic Review of the Therapeutic Effects of Reiki. *The Journal of Alternative & Complementary Medicine,* 15 (11), 1157–69.

Watson, J. (2002). Intentionality and Caring-Healing Consciousness: A Practice of Transpersonal Nursing. *Holistic Nursing Practice* 16 (4), 12–19.

Williams, C.; Dutton, D.; Burgess, C. (2010). Communicating the Intangible: A Phenomenological Exploration of Energy Healing. *Qualitative Research in Psychology,* 7, 45–56.

Yanick, P. (2006). Activate Multiple Levels of Innate Communication to Eliminate Inflammation and Pain. *The American Chiropractor,* April 2006, 42–46.

Zahourek, R. P. (2004). Intentionality Forms the Matrix of Healing: A Theory. *Alternative Therapies,* 10 (6), 40–49.

Chapter 4: Telepathy

Brassard, G.; Broadbent, A.; Tapp, A. (2005). Quantum Pseudo-Telepathy. *Foundations of Physics,* 35 (11), 1877–907.

Brownstein, D. (2011). On the Physical Basis of ESP and Telepathy. *Journal of Spirituality & Paranormal Studies,* 34 (2), 73–83.

Gisin, N.; Methot, A. A.; Scarani, V. (2007). Pseudo-Telepathy: Input Cardinality and Bell-Type Inequalities. *International Journal of Quantum Information,* 5 (4), 525–34.

Haas, A. S. (2011). The Interpretation of Telepathy Like Effects: A Novel Electromagnetic and Synchronistic Version of the Psychoanalytic Model. *NeuroQuantology*, 9 (1), 22–35.

Morse, D. R. (2009). The Evidence for Telepathy. *Journal of Spirituality & Paranormal Studies*, 32 (2), 61–62.

Piore, A. (2011). Silent Warrior. *Discover*, 32 (3), 48–76.

Powell, D. H. (2009). Twin Telepathy and the Illusion of Separation. *Shift: At the Frontiers of Consciousness*, March–May 2009 (22), 20–25.

Radin, D. (1997). *The Conscious Universe: The Scientific Truth of Psychic Phenomena*. San Francisco, CA: HarperEdge. See particularly chapter 5, Telepathy, 61–89.

Radin, D. I.; Schlitz, M. J. (2005). Gut Feelings, Intuition, and Emotions: An Exploratory Study. *The Journal of Alternative & Complementary Medicine*, 11 (1), 85–91.

Shainberg, D. (1976). Telepathy in Psychoanalysis: An Instance. *American Journal of Psychotherapy*, 30 (3), 463–72.

Sheldrake, R. (2006). Morphic Fields. *World Futures: The Journal of General Evolution*, 62 (1/2), 31–41.

Sheldrake, R.; Avraamides, L. (2009). An Automated Test for Telepathy in Connection with Emails. *Journal of Scientific Exploration*, 23 (1), 29–36.

Sheldrake, R.; Smart, P. (2008). Investigating Scopesthesia: Attentional Transitions, Controls and Error Rates in Repeated Tests. *Journal of Scientific Exploration*, 22 (4), 517–27.

Stanescu, A. (2010). The Role of Telepathy and Clairvoyance in Criminology. *Proceedings of the 4th World Congress on the Advancement of Scholarly Research in Science, Economics, Law, & Culture*, 2010, 259–63.

Temkin, A. Y. (2011). Extrasensory Perception as a Natural, but Not Supernatural Phenomenon. *NeuroQuantology*, 9 (1), 157–65.

Chapter 5: Animal Telepathy

Copeland, S. M. (2008). Mind Readers. *Horse & Rider*, 47 (9), 64–69.

Erikson, D. L. (2011). Intuition, Telepathy, and Interspecies Communication: A Multidisciplinary Perspective. *NeuroQuantology*, 9 (1), 145–52.

Hanks, L. A. (2010). Are Pet Psychics for Real? *Dog World*, 95 (2), 32–35.

Orey, C. (2001). Psychic Connections with Your Cat. *Cats Magazine*, 57 (8), 32–35.

Sheldrake, R.; Morgana, A. Testing a Language-Using Parrot for Telepathy. *Journal of Scientific Exploration*, 17, 602–15.

Sheldrake, R. (2011). *Dogs That Know When Their Owners Are Coming Home and Other Unexplained Powers of Animals*, 2nd ed. New York, NY: Crown Publishing Group.

Williams, C.; Dutton, D. (2010). What the Animals Have to Say: Conceptual Frameworks, Commonalities and Tensions in Professional Animal Psi Research and Lay-Animal Psychic Communication. *Journal of the Society for Psychical Research*, 74 (899), 94–177.

Wiseman, R.; Smith, M.; Milton, J. (1998). Can Animals Detect When Their Owners Are Returning Home? An Experimental Test of the "Psychic Pet" Phenomenon. *British Journal of Psychology*, 89 (3), 453–62.

Chapter 6: Precognition

Burns, J. E. (2006). The Arrow of Time and the Action of the Mind at the Molecular Level. In *Frontiers of Time, Retrocausation—Experiment and Theory*, D. P. Sheehan, ed. American Institute of Physics, 75–88.

Carpenter, J. (2010). Laboratory Psi Effects May Be Put to Practical Use: Two Pilot Studies. *Journal of Scientific Exploration*, 24 (4), 667–90.

Cramer, J. G. (2006). Reverse Causation and the Transactional Interpretation of Quantum Mechanics. In *Frontiers of Time, Retrocausation—Experiment and Theory*, D. P. Sheehan, ed. American Institute of Physics, 20–26.

Dobyns, Y. H. (2006). Retrocausal Information Flow: What Are the Consequences of Knowing the Future? *AIP Conference Proceedings*, 863 (1), 273–92.

Dotta, B. T.; Persinger, M. A. (2009). Dreams, Time Distortion, and the Experience of Future Events: A Relativistic, Neuroquantal Perspective. *Sleep & Hypnosis*, 11 (2), 29–39.

Nelson, R. D.; Dunne, B. J.; Dobyns, Y. H.; Jahn, R. G. (1996). Precognitive Remote Perception: Replication of Remote Viewing. *Journal of Scientific Exploration*, 10 (1), 109–10.

Radin, D. (1997). *The Conscious Universe: The Scientific Truth of Psychic Phenomena*. San Francisco, CA: HarperEdge. See particularly chapter 7, Perception through Time, 111–26.

Rauscher, E. A.; Targ, R. (2006). Investigation of a Complex Space-Time Metric to Describe Precognition of the Future. *AIP Conference Proceedings*, 863 (1), 121–46.

Roney-Dougal, S. M.; Solfvin, J. (2011). Exploring the Relationship between Tibetan Meditation Attainment and Precognition. *Journal of Scientific Exploration*, 25 (1), 29–46.

Chapter 7: Survival after Death

Agrillo, C. (2011). Near-Death Experience: Out-of-Body and Out-of-Brain? *Review of General Psychology*, 15 (1), 1–10.

Badham, P. (1997). Religious and Near-Death Experience in Relation to Belief in a Future Life. *Mortality*, 2 (1), 7–21.

Beichler, J. E. (2007). Let There Be Light: The Scientific Bleep on the Afterlife. *Journal of Spirituality & Paranormal Studies*, July 2007 Proceedings Supplement, 30, 171–179.

Beischel, J. (2007). Talking to the Dead: Laboratory Investigation of Mediumship. *Shift: At the Frontiers of Consciousness*, December 2007–February 2008, (17), 20–24.

Beischel, J.; Schwartz, G. E. (2007). Anomalous Information Reception by Research Mediums Demonstrated Using a Novel Triple-Blind Protocol. *Journal of Science and Healing*, 3 (1), 23–27.

Beischel, J.(2007). Contemporary Methods Used in Laboratory-Based Mediumship Research. *Journal of Parapsychology*, 71, 37–68.

Beischel, J.; Rock, A. J. (2009). Addressing the Survival versus Psi Debate Through Process-Focused Mediumship Research. *Journal of Parapsychology*, 73, 71–90.

Bering, J. M. (2002). Intuitive Conceptions of Dead Agents' Mind: The Natural Foundations of Afterlife Beliefs as Phenomenological Boundary. *Journal of Cognition & Culture*, 2 (4), 263–308.

Betty, L. S. (2006). Are They Hallucinations or Are They Real? The Spirituality of Deathbed and Near-Death Visions. *Omega*, 53 (1–2), 37–49.

Boccuzzi, M.; Beischel, J. (2011). Objective Analyses of Reported Real-Time Audio Instrumental Transcommunication and Matched Control Sessions: A Pilot Study. *Journal of Scientific Exploration*, 25 (2), 215–35.

Carter, C. (2010). *Science and the Near-Death Experience.* Rochester, VT: Inner Traditions.

Flannelly, K. J.; Ellison, C. G.; Galek, K.; Koenig, H. G. (2008). Beliefs about Life-After-Death, Psychiatric Symptomology and Cognitive Theories of Psychopathology. *Journal of Psychology & Theology*, 36 (2), 94–103.

Fontana, D. (2008). Disbelief Despite the Evidence. *Shift: At the Frontiers of Consciousness*, December 2007–February 2008 (17), 25–29.

Greyson, B. (1999). Defining Near-Death Experiences. *Mortality*, 4 (1), 7–19.

Greyson, B. (2005). "False Positive" Claims of Near-Death Experiences and "False Negative" Denials of Near-Death Experiences. *Death Studies*, 29, 145–55.

Greyson, B. (2006). Near-Death Experiences and Spirituality. *Zygon*, 41 (2), 393–414.

Greyson, B. (2008). The Near-Death Experience. *Alternative Therapies*, 14 (3), 14.

Greyson, B. (2008b). The Mystical Impact of Near-Death Experiences. *Shift: At the Frontiers of Consciousness*, December 2007–February 2008 (17), 8–13.

Greyson, B. (2010). Implication of Near-Death Experiences for a Postmaterialist Psychology. *Psychology of Religion and Spirituality*, 2 (1), 37–45.

Griffith, L. J. (2009). Near-Death Experiences and Psychotherapy. *Psychiatry*, 6 (10), 35–42.

Haraldsson, E. (2006). Popular Psychology, Belief in Life after Death and Reincarnation in the Nordic Countries, Western and Eastern Europe. *Nordic Psychology*, 58 (2), 171–80.

Hodge, K. M. (2008). Descartes' Mistake: How Afterlife Beliefs Challenge the Assumption That Humans Are Intuitive Cartesian Substance Dualists. *Journal of Cognition & Culture*, 8 (3/4), 387–415.

Hogan, R. C. (2009). Applying the Science of the Afterlife. *Journal of Spirituality & Paranormal Studies*, 32 (1), 6–23.

Kaufman, M. ; Kuzma, C. (2008). What Really Happens in Near-Death Experiences? *Shift: At the Frontiers of Consciousness*. Winter 2008–2009 (21), 35.

Kelly, E. W. (2001). Near-Death Experiences with Reports of Meeting Deceased People. *Death Studies*, 25, 229–249.

Lange, R.; Greyson, B.; Houran, J. (2004). A Rasch Scaling Validation of a "Core" Near-Death Experience. *British Journal of Psychology*, 95, 161–77.

Lewis, M. (2009). Is There Life after Death? *Applied Developmental Science*, 13 (3), 149–52.

Lynn, S. J.; Cleere, C.; Accardi, M.; Krackow, E. (2010). Near-Death Experiences: Out of Body and Out of Mind? *Psychology of Religion & Spirituality*, 2 (2), 117–18.

Malcom, N. L. (2010/2011). Images of Heaven and the Spiritual Afterlife: Qualitative Analysis of Children's Storybooks about Death, Dying, Grief, and Bereavement. *Omega: Journal of Death & Dying*, 62 (1), 51–76.

Melnyk, V. (2007). "But I Was Dead": Sassoon and Graves on Life after Death. *Renascence*, 60 (1), 17–31.

Meredith, F. (22 March 2011). Going into the Light. *The Irish Times*, 22 March 2011.

Moody, R. A. (1977). Is There Life after Death? *The Saturday Evening Post*, May/June 1977, 66–67, 82–85.

Morse, D. R. (2005). Can Science Prove the Soul, the Afterlife, and God? *Journal of Religion & Psychical Research*, 28 (3), 154–76.

Novak, P. (2000). Death Is Not a Door: The Re-Emergence of the Ancient Binary Soul Doctrine in Analytical Psychology and Neuropsychology and Its Implications for Our Religious and Cultural Conceptions of the Afterlife: Part 1. *Journal of Religion & Psychical Research*, 23 (3), 156–66.

O'Dowd, N. (23 March 2011). A Glimpse at the Afterlife? What Dying Patients See and Feel—New Irish Study Gives Fascinating Insights into the Last Moments. *The Irish Times*, 23 March 2011. Web: *http://www.irishcentral.com/story/news/periscope/a-glimpse-at-the-afterlife-what-dying-patients-see-and-feel--new-irish-study-gives-fascinating-insights-into-the-last-moments- 118567024.html?commentspage=2.*

Rock, A. J.; Beischel, J. (2008). Quantitative Analysis of Research Mediums' Conscious Experiences During a Discarnate Reading vs. a Control Task: A Pilot Study. *Australian Journal of Parapsychology*, 8 (2), 157–79.

Rock, A. J.; Beischel, J.; Cott, C. C. (2009). Psi vs. Survival: A Qualitative Investigation of Mediums' Phenomenology Comparing Psychic Readings and Ostensible Communication with the Deceased. *Transpersonal Psychology Review*, 13 (2), 76–89

Rock, A. J.; Beischel, J.; Schwartz, G. E. (2008). Thematic Analysis of Research Mediums' Experiences of Discarnate Communication. *Journal of Scientific Exploration*, 22 (2), 179–92.

Rock, A. J.; Beischel, J.; Schwartz, G. E. (2009). Is There Madness in Our Mediumship Methods? A Response to Roxburgh and Roe. *Journal of Scientific Exploration*, 23 (3), 351–57.

Roxburgh, E. C.; Roe, C. A. (2009). Thematic Analysis of Mediums' Experiences. *Journal of Scientific Exploration*, 23 (3), 348–51.

Schwartz, G. (2002). *The Afterlife Experiments: Breakthrough Scientific Evidence of Life after Death.* New York, NY: Pocket Books.

Siegel, R. K. (1980). The Psychology of Life After Death. *American Psychologist*, 35 (10), 911–31.

Strubelt, S. (2008). The Near-Death Experience: A Cerebellar Method to Protect Body and Soul—Lessons from the Iboga Healing Ceremony in Gabon. *Alternative Therapies*, 14 (1), 30–34.

Tan, K. A. C. (2000). The Near-Death Experience: A Glimpse of a Positive Life after Death. *LILLIPOH*, Fall 2000, 48–49.

Tart, C. T. (2007). What Death Tells Us about Life. *Shift: At the Frontiers of Consciousness*, December 2007–February 2008, (17), 30–35.

Van Lommel, P.; van Wees, R.; Meyers, V.; Elfferich, I. (2001). Near-Death Experience in Survivors of Cardiac Arrest: A Prospective Study in the Netherlands. *Lancet*, 358, 2039–45.

Vess, M.; Routledge, C.; Landau, M. J.; Arndt, J. (2009). The Dynamics of Death and Meaning: The Effects of Death-Relevant Cognitions and Personal Need for Structure on Perceptions of Meaning in Life. *Journal of Personality & Social Psychology*, 97 (4), 728–44.

Wilde, D. J.; Murray, C. D. (2009). The Evolving Self: Finding Meaning in Near-Death Experiences Using Interpretive Phenomenological Analysis. *Mental Health, Religion & Culture*, 12 (3), 223–39.

Wilfand, Y. (2009). Aramaic Tombstones from Zoar and Jewish Conceptions of the Afterlife. *Journal for the Study of Judaism: In the Persian & Hellenistic & Roman Period*, 40 (4/5), 510–39.

Wright, S. H. (2006). Clues to the Nature of the Afterlife from After-Death Communication. *Journal of Spirituality & Paranormal Studies*, 29 (3), 149–59.

Chapter 8: Past Lives and Reincarnation

Bache, C. (2006). Reincarnation and the Akashic Field: A Dialogue with Ervin Laszlo. *World Futures: The Journal of General Evolution*, 62 (1/2), 114–26.

Burris, C.T.; Bailey, K. (2009). What Lies Beyond: Theory and Measurement of Afterdeath Beliefs. *International Journal for the Psychology of Religion*, 19 (3), 173–86.

Davidson, J. R. T.; Connor, K. M.; Lee, L-C. (2005). Beliefs in Karma and Reincarnation among Survivors of Violent Trauma. *Social Psychiatry & Psychiatric Epidemiology*, 40 (2), 120–25.

Dunlap, J. W. (2007). Reincarnation and Survival of Life after Death: "Is There Evidence That Past Life Memories Suggest Reincarnation?" *Journal of Spirituality & Paranormal Studies*, 30 (Proceedings Supplement), 157–70.

Goswami, A. (2001). *Physics of the Soul: The Quantum Book of Living, Dying, Reincarnation, and Immortality*. Charlottesville, VA: Hampton Roads Publishing.

Gupta, A. (2002). Reliving Childhood? The Temporality of Childhood and Narratives of Reincarnation. *Ethnos: Journal of Anthropology*, 67 (1), 33–55.

Haraldsson, E. (2008). Persistence of Past-Life Memories: Study of Adults Who Claimed in Their Childhood to Remember a Past Life. *Journal of Scientific Exploration*, 22 (3), 385–94.

Keil, J. (2010). Questions of the Reincarnation Type. *Journal of Scientific Exploration*, 24 (1), 79–99.

Keil, J. (2010). A Case of the Reincarnation Type in Turkey Suggesting Strong Paranormal Information Involvements. *Journal of Scientific Exploration*, 24 (1), 71–77.

Keil, J.; Tucker, J. B. (2010). Response to "How to Improve the Study and Documentation of Cases of the Reincarnation Type? A Reappraisal of the Case of Kemal Atasoy." *Journal of Scientific Exploration*, 24 (2), 295–96.

Laszlo, E. (2003). *The Connectivity Hypothesis: Foundations of an Integral Science of Quantum, Cosmos, Life, and Consciousness*. Albany, NY: SUNY Press.

Laszlo, E. (2004). *Science and the Akashic Field: An Integral Theory of Everything.* Rochester, VT: Inner Traditions International.

Rivas, T. (2005). Rebirth and Personal Identity: Is Reincarnation an Intrisically Impersonal Concept? *Journal of Religion & Psychical Research*, 28 (4), 226–33.

Snider, A. (2007). The Pre-Existence of the Soul: An Argument for Reincarnation. *Journal of Spirituality & Paranormal Studies*, 30 (2), 77–79.

Stevenson, I. (1970). Characteristics of Cases of the Reincarnation Type in Turkey and Their Comparison with Cases in Two Other Cultures. *International Journal of Comparative Sociology*, 11 (1), 1–17.

Tibetan Review (2010). Dalai Lama Sure He Won't Be Reborn Under Chinese Rule. *Tibetan Review: The Monthly Magazine on All Aspects of Tibet*, 45 (8), 11.

Tucker, J. B. (2007). I've Been Here Before: Children's Reports of Previous Lives. *Shift: At the Frontiers of Consciousness*, December 2007/January 2008 (17), 14–19.

Tucker, J. B. (2005). *Life Before Life: Children's Memories of Previous Lives.* New York, NY: St. Martin's Griffin.

Visoni, V. M. (2010). How to Improve the Study and Documentation of Cases of the Reincarnation Type? A Reappraisal of the Case of Kemal Atasoy. *Journal of Scientific Exploration*, 24 (1), 101–8.

Walter, T.; Waterhouse, H. (1999). A Very Private Belief: Reincarnation in Contemporary England. *Sociology of Religion*, 60 (2), 187–97.

Wise Jr., C. C. (1992). Reincarnation Reconsidered. *Journal of Religion & Psychical Research*, 15 (1), 17–24.

Zivkovic, T. M. (2010). The Biographical Process of a Tibetan Lama. *Ethnos: Journal of Anthropology*, 75 (2), 171–89.

Other Topics

Energy and Meditation

Aiken, W. R. (1990). Kundalini. *Journal of Religion & Psychical Research,* 13 (4), 209–11.

Arambula, P.; Peper, E.; Kawakami, M.; Gibney, K. H. (2001). The Physiological Correlates of Kundalini Yoga Meditation: A Study of a Yoga Master. *Applied Psychophysiology & Biofeedback,* 26 (2), 147–53.

Cahn, B. R.; Polich, J. (2006). Meditation States and Traits: EEG, ERP, and Neuroimaging Studies. *Psychological Bulletin,* 132 (2), 180–211.

Chiesa, A. (2009). Zen Meditation: An Integration of Current Evidence. *Journal of Alternative & Complementary Medicine,* 15 (5), 585–92.

Chrism, M. (2008). Shakti and Shiva Kundalini Awakening and the Sacred Male and Female Energy. *Share Guide,* March/April 2008 (96), 89–99.

Chu, L-C. (2010). The Benefits of Meditation vis-à-vis Emotional Intelligence, Perceived Stress, and Negative Mental Health. *Stress & Health: Journal of the International Society for the Investigation of Stress,* 26 (2), 169–80.

Coward, H. G. (1985). Jung and Kundalini. *Journal of Analytical Psychology,* 30 (4), 379–92.

Davis, D. M.; Hayes, J. A. (2011). What Are the Benefits of Mindfulness? A Practice Review of Psychotherapy-Related Research. *Psychotherapy.* 48 (2), 198–208.

Edson, C. J. (1991). Kundalini: Is It Real? *Journal of Religion & Psychical Research,* 14 (1), 27–43.

Engstrom, M.; Pihlsgard, J.; Lundberg, P.; Soderfeldt, B. (2010). Functional Magnetic Resonance Imaging of Hippocampal Activation During Silent Mantra Meditation. *Journal of Alternative & Complementary Medicine.* 16 (12), 1253–58.

Goyal, M.; Haythornthwaite, J.; Levine, D.; Becker, D.; Vaidya, D.; Hill-Briggs, F.; Ford, D. (2010). Intensive Meditation for

Refractory Pain and Symptoms. *Journal of Alternative & Complementary Medicine*, 16 (6), 627–31.

Halsbad, U.; Mueller, S.; Hinterberger, T.; Strickner, S. (2009). Plasticity Changes in the Brain in Hypnosis and Meditation. *Contemporary Hypnosis*, 26 (4), 194–215.

Khalsa, S. S.; Rudraug, D.; Damasio, A. R.; Davidson, R. J.; Lutz, A.;Tranel, D. (2008). Interoceptive Awareness of Experienced Meditators. *Psychophysiology*, 45 (4), 671–77.

Krisanaprakomkit, T.; Sriraj, W.; Piyavhatkul, N.; Laopaiboon, M. (2008). Meditation Therapy for Anxiety Disorders. *Cochrane Database of Systematic Reviews*, 10 November 2008.

Krisanaprakomkit, T.; Ngamjarus, C.; Witoonchart, C.; Piyavhatkul, N. (2010). Meditation Therapies for Attention-Deficit/Hyperactivity Disorder (ADHD). *Cochrane Database of Systematic Reviews*, 11 May 2010.

Kumar, R. (2002). How Shakti-Kundalini Conquers Death Anxiety and Achieves Liberation. *Journal of Religion & Psychical Research*, 25 (2), 63–75.

Kumar, R.; Dempsey, M. (2002). Kundalini, Soul and the Right Side of the Brain. *Journal of Religion & Psychical Research*, 25 (3), 148–57.

Lagopoulos, J.; Xu, J.; Rasmussen, I.; Vik, A.; Malhi, G. S.; Eliassen, C. F.; Amtsen, I. E.; Saether, J. G.; Hollup, S.; Hoeln, A.; et al. (2009). Increased Theta and Alpha EEG Activity During Nondirective Meditation. *Journal of Alternative & Complementary Medicine*, 15 (11), 1187–92.

Lavallee, C., F.; Koren, S. A.; Persinger, M. A. (2011). A Quantitative Electroencephalographic Study of Meditation and Binaural Beat Entrainment. *Journal of Alternative & Complementary Medicine*, 17 (4), 351–55.

Lewis, N. (1996). Serpent of Fire: A Modern View of Kundalini. *Noetic Sciences Review*, Spring 1996, (37), 41–43.

Marshall, P. (2011). The Psychical and the Mystical: Boundaries, Connections, Common Origins. *Journal of the Society for Psychical Research*, 75 (902), 1–13.

Maxwell, R. W. (2009). The Physiological Foundation of Yoga Chakra Expression. *Zygon: Journal of Religion & Science*, 44 (4), 807–24.

Mohan, A.; Sharma, R.; Bijlani, R. L. (2011). Effect of Meditation on Stress-Induced Changes in Cognitive Functions. *Journal of Alternative & Complementary Medicine*, 17 (3), 207–12.

Naura, H. (2004). Rousing the Kundalini. *The Journal of Yoga*, 3 (2), 1–3.

Nelson, J. E. (1994). Madness or Transcendence? Looking to the Ancient East for a Modern Transpersonal Diagnostic System. *ReVision*, 17 (1), 14–23.

Ospina, M. B.; Bond, K.; Karkhaneh, M.; Buscemi, N.; Dryden, D. M.; Barnes, V.; Carlson, L. E.; Dusek, J. A.; Shannahoff-Khalsa, D. (2008). Clinical Trials of Meditation Practices in Health Care: Characteristics and Quality. *Journal of Alternative & Complementary Medicine*, 14 (10), 1199–213.

Roney-Dougal, S. M.; Solfvin, J. (2011). Exploring the Relationship between Tibetan Meditation Attainment and Precognition. *Journal of Scientific Exploration*, 25 (1), 29–46.

Schmeidler, G. R. (1990). Questions and Comments on Kundalini Research. *Journal of Religion & Psychical Research*, 13 (1), 43–46.

Shannaahoff-khalsa, D. S. (2003). Kundalini Yoga Meditation Techniques for the Treatment of Obsessive-Compulsive and OC Spectrum Disorders. *Brief Treatment & Crisis Intervention*, 3 (3), 369–82.

Shannaahoff-khalsa, D. S. (2004). An Introduction to Kundalini Yoga Meditation Techniques That Are Specific for the Treatment of Psychiatric Disorders. *Journal of Alternative & Complementary Medicine*, 10 (1), 91–101.

Sharma, M. (2001). Pilot Test of a Kundalini-Yoga Intervention Developing the Mind-Body Connection. *International Journal of Yoga Therapy*, 2001, (11), 85–91.

Shulman, L. (2007). Revealing the Chakras. *Alive: Canada's National Health & Wellness Magazine*, April 2007 (294), 110–11.

Wachholtz, A. B.; Pargament, K. I. (2008). Migraines and Meditation: Does Spirituality Matter? *Journal of Behavioral Medicine*, 31 (4), 351–66.

Wisner, B. L.; Jones, B.; Gwin, D. (2010). School-Based Meditation Practices for Adolescents: A Resource for Strengthening Self-Regulation, Emotional Coping, and Self-Esteem. *Children & Schools*. 32 (3), 150–59.

Zeidan, F.; Johnson, S. K.; Gordon, N. S.; Goolkasian, P. (2010). Effects of Brief and Sham Mindfulness Meditation on Mood and Cardiovascular Variables. *Journal of Alternative & Complementary Medicine*, 16 (8), 867–73.

Out-of-Body Experiences

Ananthaswamy, A. The Mind Unshackled. *New Scientist*, 204 (2729), 34–36.

De Ridder, D.; Van Laere, K.; Dupont, P.; Menovsky, T.; Van de Heyning, P. (2007). Visualizing Out-of-Body Experience in the Brain. *The New England Journal of Medicine*, 357 (18), 1829–33.

Fracasso, C.; Friedman, H. (2011). Near Death Experiences and the Possibility of Disembodied Consciousness. *NeuroQuantology*, 9 (1), 41–53.

Kotter, S. (2005). Extreme States. *Discover*, 26 (7), 60–67.

Laws, V.; Perry, E. (2010). Near Death Experiences: A New Algorithmic Approach to Verifying Consciousness Outside the Brain. *NeuroQuantology*, 8 (2), 142–54.

Meyerson, J.; Gelkopf, M. (2004). Therapeutic Utilization of Spontaneous Out-of-Body Experiences in Hypnotherapy. *American Journal of Psychotherapy*, 58 (1), 90-102.

Murray, C. D.; Fox, J. (2005). Dissociational Body Experiences: Differences between Respondents with and without Prior Out-of-Body Experiences. *British Journal of Psychology*, 96 (4), 441–56.

Neppe, V. M. (2011). Models of the Out of Body Experience: A new Multi Etiological Phenomenological Approach. *NeuroQuantology*, 9 (1), 72–83.

Persinger, M. A. (2010). The Harribance Effect as Pervasive Out-of-Body Experience: NeuroQuantal Evidence with More Precise Measurements, *NeuroQuantology*, 8 (4), 444–64.

Saroka, K.; Mulligan, B. P.; Murphy, T. R.; Persinger, M. A. (2010). Experimental Elicitation of an Out of Body Experience and Concomitment Cross-Hemispheric Electroencephalographic Coherence. *NeuroQuantology*, 8 (4), 466–77.

Wilde, D.; Murray, C. D. (2010). Interpreting the Anomalous: Finding Meaning in Out of Body and Near-Death Experiences. *Qualitative Research in Psychology*, 7 (1), 57–72.

Zingrone, N. L.; Alvarado, C. S.; Agee, N. (2009). Psychological Correlates of Aura Vision: Psychic Experiences, Dissociation, Absorption, and Synaesthesia-Like Experiences. *Australian Journal of Clinical & Experimental Hypnosis*, 37 (2), 131–68.

Psychic Phenomena—General

Anthony, M. (2008). The Case for Integrated Intelligence. *World Futures: The Journal of General Evolution*, 64 (4), 233–53.

Braud, W. G. (1992). Human Interconnectedness: Research Indications. *ReVision* 14 (3), 140–48.

Caudill, M. (2006). *Suddenly Psychic: A Skeptic's Journey*. Charlottesville, VA: Hampton Roads Publishing.

Cigale, E. (2009). The Value of the Transpersonal in Psychotherapy and in Everyday Life. *Europe's Journal of Psychology*, Special Section February 2009, 1–16.

Keen, J. S. (2009). A Model of Consciousness. *World Futures: The Journal of General Evolution*, 65 (4), 225–40.

Lavallee, C. F.; Koren, S. A.; Persinger, M. A. (2011). A Quantitative Electroencephalographic Study of Meditation and Binaural Beat Entrainment. *Journal of Alternative & Complementary Medicine*, 17 (4), 351–55.

Murphy, T. R. (2010). The Role of Religious and Mystic Experiences in Human Evolution: A Corollary Hypothesis for NeuroTheology. *NeuroQuantology*, 8 (4), 495–508.

Neppe, V. M. (2011). Ensuring Homogeneous Data Collection for Present and Future Research on Possible Psi Phenomena by Detailing Subjective Descriptions, Using the Multi-Axial A to Z SEATTLE Classification. *NeuroQuantology*, 9 (1), 84–105.

Persinger, M. A.; Corradini, P. L.; Clement, A. L.; Keaney, C. C.; MacDonald, M. L; Meltz, L. I.; Murugan, N. J.; Poirier, M. R.; Punkkinen, K. A.; Rossini, M. C.; Thompson, S. E. (2010). NeuroTheology and Its Convergence with NeuroQuantology. *NeuroQuantology*, 8 (4), 432–43.

Pierre, L.; Persinger, M. (2006). Experimental Facilitation of the Sensed Presence is Predicted by the Specific Patterns of the Applied Magnetic Fields, Not by Suggestibility: Reanalysis of 19 Experiments. *International Journal of Neuroscience*, 116 (9), 1079–96.

Ryan, A. (2008). New Insights into the Links between ESP and Geomagnetic Activity. *Journal of Scientific Exploration*, 22 (3), 335-358.

Srinivasan, M. (2007). Bridging the Gap between Science and Spirituality: The Role of Scientific Investigations of Paranormal Phenomena. *Electronic Journal of Sociology,*, 2007, 1–9.

Storm, L.; Tressoldi, P. E.; Di Risio, L. (2010). Meta-analysis of Free-Response Studics, 1992–2008: Assessing the Noise Reduction Model in Parapsychology. *Psychological Bulletin*, 136 (4), 471–85.

Targ, R.; Katra J. (2001). The Scientific and Spiritual Implications of Psychic Abilities. *Alternative Therapies in Health and Medicine*, 7 (3), 143–49.

Wayne, M. (2006). Consciousness and Nonlocality. *Alternative Therapies in Health & Medicine*, 12 (6), 64–67.

Recommended Books

Beauregard, M.; O'Leary, D. (2007). *The Spiritual Brain: A Neuroscientist's Case for the Existence of the Soul.* New York, NY: HarperOne.

Buchanan, L. (2003). *The Seventh Sense: The Secrets of Remote Viewing as told by a "Psychic Spy" for the U.S. Military.* New York, NY: Paraview Pocket Books.

Botkin, A. L. (2005). *Induced After Death Communication: A New Therapy for Healing Grief and Trauma.* Charlottesville, VA: Hampton Roads Publishing.

Bruce, R. (2009). *Astral Dynamics: The Complete Book of Out-of-Body Experiences.* Charlottesville, VA: Hampton Roads Publishing.

Bruce, R. (2011). *Energy Work: The Secret of Healing and Spiritual Development.* Charlottesville, VA: Hampton Roads Publishing.

Bruce, R. (2011). *The Practical Psychic Self Defense Handbook: A Survival Guide.* Charlottesville, VA: Hampton Roads Publishing.

Carter, C. (2010). *Science and the Near-Death Experience.* Rochester, VT: Inner Traditions.

Caudill, M. (2006). *Suddenly Psychic: A Skeptic's Journey.* Charlottesville, VA: Hampton Roads Publishing.

D'Souza, D. (2009). *Life after Death: The Evidence.* Washington, DC: Regnery Publishing, Inc.

Druckman, D.; Swets, J. A. (Editors). (1988). *Enhancing Human Performance: Issues, Theories, and Techniques.* Washington, DC: National Academy Press.

Gerber, R. (2000). *A Practical Guide to Vibrational Medicine: Energy Healing and Spiritual Transformation.* New York, NY: HarperCollins Publishers.

Goswami, A. (2008). *God Is Not Dead: What Quantum Physics Tells Us about Our Origins and How We Should Live.* Charlottesville, VA: Hampton Roads Publishing.

Goswami, A. (2011). *The Quantum Doctor: A Quantum Physicist Explains the Healing Power of Integral Medicine,* revised ed. Charlottesville, VA: Hampton Roads Publishing.

Kamenetz, R. (2007). *The History of Last Night's Dream: Discovering the Hidden Path to the Soul.* New York, NY: HarperOne.

Krishna, G. (1997). *Kundalini: The Evolutionary Energy in Man.* Boston, MA: Shambhala Publications.

Laszlo, E. (2003). The Connectivity Hypothesis: Foundations of an Integral Science of Quantum, Cosmos, Life, and Consciousness. Albany, NY: SUNY Press.

Laszlo, E. (2004). *Science and the Akashic Field: An Integral Theory of Everything.* Rochester, VT: Inner Traditions International.

Lipton, B. (2005). *The Biology of Belief: Unleashing the Power of Consciousness, Matter, and Miracles.* Santa Rosa, CA: Mountain of Love.

Long, J.; Perry, P. (2010). *Evidence of the Afterlife: The Science of Near-Death Experiences.* New York, NY: HarperCollins.

McMoneagle, J. (1997). *Mind Trek: Exploring Consciousness, Time, and Space Through Remote Viewing.* Charlottesville, VA: Hampton Roads Publishing.

McMoneagle, J. (1998). *The Ultimate Time Machine: A Remote Viewer's Perception of Time, and Predictions for the New Millennium.* Charlottesville, VA: Hampton Roads Publishing.

McMoneagle, J. (2000). *Remote Viewing Secrets: A Handbook.* Charlottesville, VA: Hampton Roads Publishing.

McMoneagle, J. (2002). *The Stargate Chronicles: Memoirs of a Psychic Spy.* Charlottesville, VA: Hampton Roads Publishing.

Mishlove, J. (2000). *The PK Man: A True Story of Mind over Matter.* Charlottesville, VA: Hampton Roads Publishing.

Moody, R. A. (1988). *The Light Beyond: New Explorations by the Author of Life after Life.* New York, NY: Bantam.

Radin, D. (2006). *Entangled Minds: Extrasensory Experiences in a Quantum Reality.* New York: Paraview Books.

Radin, D. (1997). *The Conscious Universe: The Scientific Truth of Psychic Phenomena.* San Francisco, CA: HarperEdge.

Schwartz, G. (2002). *The Afterlife Experiments: Breakthrough Scientific Evidence of Life after Death.* New York, NY: Pocket Books.

Schwartz, G. (2011). *The Sacred Promise: How Science Is Discovering Spirit's Collaboration with Us in Our Daily Lives.* New York, NY: Atria Books.

Sheldrake, R. (2011). *Dogs That Know When Their Owners Are Coming Home: And Other Unexplained Powers of Animals.* New York, NY: Crown Publishing Group.

Sheldrake, R. (1981). *A New Science of Life.* Los Angeles, CA: J. P. Tarcher.

Sheldrake, R.. (1988). *The Presence of the Past.* New York, NY: Vintage.

Sheldrake, R. (1991). *The Rebirth of Nature.* New York, NY: Bantam.

Sheldrake, R. (2002). *Seven Experiments That Could Change the World: A Do-It-Yourself Guide to Revolutionary Science,* 2nd ed. Rochester, VT: Park Street Press.

Sheldrake, R. (2003). *The Sense of Being Stared At: And Other Aspects of the Extended Mind.* New York, NY: Crown Publishers.

Smith, P. H. (2005). *Reading the Enemy's Mind: Inside Star Gate— America's Psychic Espionage Program.* New York, NY: Forge Press.

Strassman, R. (2001). *DMT: The Spirit Molecule; A Doctor's Revolutionary Research into the Biology of Near-Death and Mystical Experience.* Rochester, VT: Park Street Press.

Swann, I. (1996). *Remote Viewing: The Real Story, An Autobiographical Memoir.* Web e-book, partial manuscript available at *http://www.biomindsuperpowers.com/Pages/2.html.*

Talbot, M. (1991). *The Holographic Universe.* New York, NY: Harper Perennial.

Tart, C. T. (2009). *The End of Materialism: How Evidence of the Paranormal Is Bringing Science and Spirit Together.* Oakland, CA: New Harbinger Publications in association with Noetic Books.

Tucker, J. B. (2005). *Life before Life: Children's Memories of Previous Lives.* New York, NY: St. Martin's Griffin.

Van Lommel, P. (2010). *Consciousness beyond Life: The Science of the Near-Death Experience.* Translated by L. Vroomen from 2007 Dutch edition, *Eindeloos Bewustzijn.* New York, NY: HarperOne.

Resources If You
Want to Learn More

For those wishing to learn more directly about psychic phenomena, or even learn how to access their own psychic selves, I recommend the following websites and resources.

The first place to check is my website (*www.MaureenCaudill.com*).

General Psychic Training and Information

The Monroe Institute

www.monroeinstitute.org

For general training on how to access altered states of consciousness, I can recommend no better place than the Monroe Institute, Faber, Virginia (affectionately called TMI). Their original technology, Hemi-Sync, has been tested for more than forty years and is safe, reliable, and highly effective at training people—even those with no prior meditative experience—to achieve altered states of consciousness in which various psychic skills can be accessed. Their new technology, SAM, or Spatial Angle Modulation, shows promise to be even more effective and equally as safe. TMI is where I received much of my training. It offers a dozen or more residential programs, from Gateway, the starting point for the other programs, to programs in manifesting and manipulating physical objects, doing energy healing, accessing spiritual guidance, and much, much more. If you are interested in exploring a new part of yourself, TMI gets my highest recommendation as the place to start.

Association for Research and Enlightenment (ARE)

www.edgarcayce.org

This institute was founded by renowned mystic Edgar Cayce. Its headquarters are in Virginia Beach, Virginia. The institute has archives of Cayce's predictions and offers some excellent workshops and conferences throughout the year at their wonderful facilities.

Remote Viewing

Many training programs are available, but the effective ones—and the best ones—may be fairly expensive. Recommended resources are noted below. Note the importance of selecting a training program that keeps to a strict protocol, but which does not force a rigid methodology on you. The Monroe Institute's remote-viewing one-week intensive, which was developed by Skip Atwater, and which is where I received my training, is no longer offered by the institute.

International Remote Viewing Association (IRVA)

www.irva.org

For those interested in remote viewing, this organization was founded by the most experienced people involved in developing remote viewing for the military and intelligence organizations, including Ingo Swann (the "father" of remote viewing), Hal Puthoff, Russell Targ, Skip Atwater, and many others. This is the authoritative place for serious remote viewers for information about remote viewing, conferences, and so on.

Lyn Buchanan's Controlled Remote Viewing Training and Services

www.crviewer.com

Lyn Buchanan, one of the original military "psychic spies," has developed a training program in "controlled" remote viewing. This is one of several specific methodologies, but it's taught by someone who genuinely knows what he's doing.

Hawaii Remote Viewers' Guild

www.hrvg.org/training.php

The Hawaii Remote Viewers' Guild is a nonprofit organization that offers online training for preliminary remote viewers, followed by residential training for the most advanced techniques. The methodology presented tends to be fairly rigid; however, some superb remote viewers have come out of this program.

Healing

Matrix Energetics

www.matrixenergetics.com

Richard Bartlett developed an interesting healing methodology called Matrix Energetics and has gathered a substantial following throughout the country. His seminars are primarily (but not solely) taught on the West Coast, but he does teach in other locations on occasion.

Bradford Keeney

www.mojodoctors.com

Bradford Keeney offers training in a shamanic-like shaking medicine using dance to achieve healing states.

Animal Communications

Penelope Smith

www.animaltalk.net

Penelope Smith is one of the best animal communicators out there, and she not only provides readings but also has generated advice on how to hire an animal communicator and provides a code of ethics. She maintains a directory of animal communicators all over the world who agree to follow her code of ethics.

Mediums

John Edward

www.johnedward.net

John Edward is one of the most phenomenal psychic mediums of our time. It's not easy to get an appointment with him, but it is definitely worth participating in any of his events that you can manage. He's hugely popular and has been featured as the star of several television series.

Laurie Campbell

www.lauriecampbell.net/services.html

Laurie Campbell is another enormously talented spiritual medium. She has also worked as a police medium in solving crimes and has been featured in a number of television series as a police medium. Again, she is hugely talented and extremely accurate.

Near-Death Experiences

International Association for Near-Death Studies

www.iands.org/home.html

If you or any of your friends or family have experienced a near-death experience, you may want to investigate the International Association for Near-Death Studies website.

Reincarnation

University of Virginia Division of Perceptual Studies

www.medicine.virginia.edu/clinical/departments/psychiatry/
sections/cspp/dops/home-page

If you have a reincarnation story you believe to be well documented, I encourage you to contact the folks at the University of Virginia, Division of Perceptual Studies. They investigate such claims all over the world.

Out-of-Body Experiences

Astral Dynamics

www.astraldynamics.com

Robert Bruce, an Australian mystic, offers online courses in going out of the body. His books are universally excellent and offer practical, effective, and down-to-earth information on astral projection, energy work, and protecting yourself from negative psychic elements. I recommend his books and courses highly.

Notes

Introduction: Black Swans and Other Challenges to Comfortable Reality

1. Such explanations are the equivalent of the government's "weather balloon" explanation for UFOs. I personally have never seen a UFO. Furthermore, most—perhaps even 95 percent—of the reports I hear about seem easily dismissed. That said, the other 5 percent of the reports are provocative and well worth further investigation. Personally, I haven't the faintest idea what such sightings really are. But I definitely do *not* believe they are weather balloons.

2. If you have a different opinion about this, humor me anyway. It's not nice to tease the crazy people.

3. As all cat owners realize, dogs have owners, while cats have staff. I'm the staff. The difference in roles is profound.

Chapter 1: The First Black Swan: Psychokinesis

4. I should note that I don't expect people to achieve Uri Geller's level of spoon-bending in the space of the fifteen or twenty minutes I spend teaching them how to do it. Instead of asking them to soften the fork enough for it to droop and melt on its own, I merely ask them to soften it enough so that it feels like modeling clay, so they can bend and twist it however they want. I use only high-quality cutlery when I teach this; specifically I look for

18/10 stainless steel. I also test the forks to make sure I cannot bend individual tines or the fork's handle with my fingers before starting the spoon-bending procedure. If it's possible for me to bend it with my fingers before starting, it's not stiff enough to use to teach people how to spoon-bend.

5. This is also why I *never* teach spoon-bending before lunch in a workshop. I always wait to teach it right after lunch, after people have moved away from any cutlery. I take no responsibility for ruined cutlery as a result of my educational efforts. So be warned.

6. I have had the occasional very gifted student do more with spoons. One person turned the bowl of his spoon inside out. I've also had students take forks and flatten them, and then roll them up like eggrolls. Occasionally I've had one or two flatten them and stretch them, as you would stretch dough when rolling it out. People can be very inventive when spoon-bending!

7. One technique I teach people to use to ensure their intentions are firmly fixed on the fork is to tell them to yell at it: "Bend! Bend! Bend!" It's hard to let your mind wander when you're yelling something, and the energy of yelling amplifies the energy you're putting into the fork. Besides, it entertains me enormously to watch grown-up people yelling at their cutlery. Sometimes people are extremely amusing when we get to this part of the process. In the workshop with Robert Bruce, when we got to the yelling part, his girlfriend (now his wife), Patricia, had trouble yelling. She's an extremely sweet person, and I had to prod her to put her heart and soul into yelling at her fork. I just about roared with laughter when I heard her ever-so-apologetically address her fork, "Bend! I'm so sorry! I'm a Canadian! Bend!"

8. As you might have guessed, I get that "it's all a fake" comment a lot, and not just about spoon-bending. I try to graciously smile and not argue, though there are times I have an insane impulse to follow them home and bend every piece of their best silver, just to make a point. If you've irritated me, it's probably not a good idea to ask me to help with the dishes lest there be an occasional psychokinetic "accident." I'm just saying.

9. Yes, people really do that. I know someone who regularly takes groups of people to Las Vegas to a casino. They do group energy and manifestation exercises in a hotel suite upstairs, then go down to the casino and work their magic at the craps table. They limit how much they win (and donate most of the profits beyond travel expenses to a charity). The casino loves them because watching a group of people doing verbal energy exercises around a craps table is a big attention-draw for regular patrons. It increases the overall traffic in the casino, and thus, despite the relatively small wins the group makes (on the order of a few thousand dollars over a couple of evenings), the overall casino winnings increase. Casinos really do love winners because seeing someone celebrate a good-size win brings more people into the casino to lose their money. The results of the casino trips are reported regularly, and as far as I've seen, they've never come home with less than a winning result, though the amount of the win varies with the skill of the group.

10. While I'm making a point about not being irresponsible about working with psychic skills, it's also true that you shouldn't be afraid of it either. It's important to have an open mind, to "play" around with it. But do so responsibly and not with any intention of doing harm to anyone or anything.

11. Shen, D. (2010). Unexpected Behavior of Matter in Conjunction with Human Consciousness. *Journal of Scientific Exploration*, 24 (1), 41–52.

12. Shen, D. (2010). Unexpected Behavior of Matter in Conjunction with Human Consciousness. *Journal of Scientific Exploration*, 24 (1), 45.

13. Radin, D. (1997). *The Conscious Universe: The Scientific Truth of Psychic Phenomena*. San Francisco, CA: HarperEdge, 133–34.

14. Bosch, H., Steinkamp, F., Boller, E. (2006). Examining Psychokinesis: The Interaction of Human Intention with Random Number Generators—A Meta-Analysis. *Psychological Bulletin*, 132 (4), 497–523.

15. Radin, D., Nelson, R., Dobyns, Y., Houtkooper, J. (2006). Reexamining Psychokinesis: Comment on Bosch, Steinkamp, and Boller (2006). *Psychological Bulletin*, 132 (4), 529–32.

16. Radin, D., Nelson, R., Dobyns, Y., Houtkooper, J. (2006). Reexamining Psychokinesis: Comment on Bosch, Steinkamp, and Boller (2006). *Psychological Bulletin*, 132 (4), 530.

17. Bosch, H., Steinkamp, F., Biller, E. (2006). Examining Psychokinesis: The Interaction of Human Intention with Random Number Generators—A Meta-Analysis. *Psychological Bulletin*, 132 (4), 517.

18. Smith, P. H. (2005). *Reading the Enemy's Mind: Inside Star Gate— America's Psychic Espionage Program.* New York, NY: Forge Press, 31–35.

Chapter 2: The Second Black Swan: Remote Viewing

19 Yes, I know that skeptics assume that remote viewers want to be "front-loaded" with information about the target, but the exact opposite is the case. A competent remote viewer wants to know as little as possible about the target location or person prior to the remote viewing session.

20. For more details about this highly eventful "awakening," see my book *Suddenly Psychic: A Skeptic's Journey*, (Newburyport, MA: Hampton Roads Publishing, 2006).

21. This program was the "Remote Viewing Practicum" offered by the Monroe Institute for a period of time in the early 2000s. Unfortunately, this superb training program is no longer offered by the institute. While intense and exhausting in its six-day format, it was a phenomenally good remote viewing training program.

22. This is, quite frankly, the reason I don't do a lot of remote viewing. It's simply too time-consuming, and requires a lot of cooperation from several people, to follow a proper protocol.

23. As noted earlier, however, I still find that critical remote-viewing sessions are much more accurate when I use the audio signals to keep me focused. In large part, this is because I don't remote view that regularly, so I don't stay in practice at accessing the remote viewing states.

24. For example, see any of the following:

Buchanan, L. (2003). *The Seventh Sense: The Secrets of Remote Viewing as Told by a "Psychic Spy" for the U.S. Military.* New York, NY: Paraview Pocket Books.

McMoneagle, J. (2002). *The Stargate Chronicles: Memoirs of a Psychic Spy.* Charlottesville, VA: Hampton Roads Publishing.

Smith, P. H. (2005). *Reading the Enemy's Mind: Inside Star Gate— America's Psychic Espionage Program.* New York, NY: Forge Press.

Swann, I. (1996). *Remote Viewing: The Real Story, An Autobiographical Memoir.* Web e-book, partial ms. available at *www.biomindsuperpowers.com/Pages/2.html.*

25. For an in-depth explanation of the events leading up to the various investigations and reports about the military remote-viewing programs, see Paul Smith's 2005 book, *Reading the Enemy's Mind: Inside Star Gate—America's Psychic Espionage Program.* New York, NY: Forge Press.

26. Utts, J. (1996). An Assessment of the Evidence for Psychic Functioning. *Journal of Scientific Exploration,* 10 (1), 13.

27. It should be mentioned that in the nearly twenty years since this study, this conclusion has been overturned; quality training programs such as the one I attended have been developed and some are still available.

28. Utts, J. (1996). An Assessment of the Evidence for Psychic Functioning. *Journal of Scientific Exploration,* 10 (1), 22.

29. Hyman, R. (1996). Evaluation of a Program on Anomalous Mental Phenomena. *Journal of Scientific Exploration* 10 (1), 39–40.

Chapter 3: The Third Black Swan: Energy Healing

30. Shore, A. G. (2004). Long-Term Effects of Energetic Healing on Symptoms of Psychological Depression and Self-Perceived Stress. *Alternative Therapies,* 10 (3), 42–48.

31. Jackson, E., Kelley, M., McNeil, P., Meyer, E., Schlegel, L, Eaton, M. (2008). Does Therapeutic Touch Help Reduce Pain and Anxiety in Patients with Cancer? *Clinical Journal of Oncology Nursing,* 12 (1), 113–20.

32. DiNucci, E. M. (2005). Energy Healing: A Complementary Technique for Orthopaedic and Other Conditions. *Orthopaedic Nursing,* 24 (4), 259–69.

33. MacIntyre, B., Hamilton, J., Fricke, T., Ma, W., Mehle, S., Michel, M. (2008). The Efficacy of Healing Touch in Coronary Artery Bypass Surgery Recovery: A Randomized Clinical Trial. *Alternative Therapies,* 14 (4), 24–32.

34. Zahourek, R. P. (2004). Intentionality Forms the Matrix of Healing: A Theory. *Alternative Therapies,* 10 (6), 40–49.

35. Watson, J. (2002). Intentionality and Caring-Healing Consciousness: A Practice of Transpersonal Nursing. *Holistic Nursing Practice,* 16 (4), 12–19.

Chapter 4: The Fourth Black Swan: Telepathy

36. Only after the fact did I realize that one of those friends felt the emotional connection to be an invasion of privacy, even though all I got was emotion but not specifics. I did my best to close that connection once I realized that, but it took me several months to accomplish the shutdown. Again, I had no clue how to shut it down in large part because I had no clue how I'd opened that telempathic connection to begin with. Plus, I might add that it was equally as uncomfortable for me as for my friend. It's no fun feeling someone else's pain!

37. Sheldrake, R., Avraamides, L. (2009). An Automated Test for Telepathy in Connection with Emails. *Journal of Scientific Exploration*, 23 (1), 29–36.

38. Sheldrake had done an earlier series of experiments in which people predicted who was calling them on the phone (a phone without caller ID, I might add!) before they picked up. In that earlier set of studies in 2003–2004, they arranged calls to volunteers from any of four predesignated people. The person receiving the call had to predict which of the four people was calling before picking up the phone—and they were videotaped to ensure no cheating. In 271 trials, the participants correctly guessed the caller 45 percent of the time, when chance would predict 25 percent correct guesses. The probability of this experimental result being due to random chance? It was less than one in a million.

39. I have a friend who is consistently aggravated with me. She writes me a detailed email about something, and before she even has the chance to hit "Send,"I've called her on the phone. It seems to her that I almost always call her when she's in the middle of writing an email to me. It's aggravating to her because of the time she spends writing those emails. Sometimes she sends the email anyway—or refuses to tell me whatever information she put in the email so as not to have wasted her efforts writing it.

40. Even psychics can succumb to the dreary middle-of-the-task doldrums. It's a lot like a midweek slump. There's a reason Wednesday is called "hump day"!

41. Radin, D. (1997). *The Conscious Universe: The Scientific Truth of Psychic Phenomena*. San Francisco, CA: HarperEdge, 87–88. See particularly chapter 5, Telepathy, 61–89.

42. See *Suddenly Psychic*, Hampton Roads Publishing, 2006, chapter 5.

43. As if! In reality, I have no "reputation as a telepath." I'm a decent remote viewer, but not a telepath—at least not so far.

44. I should point out that when we were being briefed on how the experiment would be conducted a week or so beforehand, I specifically asked if it mattered if I didn't get information about the video clip telepathically. While I was assured it didn't matter how I detected the video clip, I also received the strong impression that the researcher did not believe anything except telepathy could possibly explain a correct description of the video clip.

Chapter 5: The Fifth Black Swan: Animal Telepathy

45. Tinkerbell also sometimes seems to insist that I call a particular person. She comes to me and engages in a very specific behavior pattern. I also receive a clear image in my mind of who it is I'm supposed to call—there's no confusion about who she means, even though her behavior is the same in all cases. This can continue for a few minutes to an hour or more, until I give in and pick up the phone. Once I reach the person she wanted me to call, I can put the phone on speakerphone and she holds an extended "conversation" with that person. Almost invariably, the person she wants me to call is upset over something and wanted to talk to someone about it. This is part of the reason I have a phone package that gives me free long-distance calling.

46. If you call me and hear what sounds like a baby squalling in the background . . . it's Tink. She has a very distinctive voice.

47. Sheldrake, R. (2011). *Dogs That Know When Their Owners Are Coming Home: And Other Unexplained Powers of Animals*, 2nd ed. New York, NY: Crown Publishing Group. See particularly chapter 2, 29–65.

48. Sheldrake, R. (2011). *Dogs That Know When Their Owners Are Coming Home: And Other Unexplained Powers of Animals*, 2nd ed. New York, NY: Crown Publishing Group, 38.

49. The same survey asked cat owners whether their cats similarly anticipated their owners' arrival home. Between 30 and 45 percent of California respondents reported positively on this

question, while only 15 to 20 percent of British cat owners gave positive responses. The lower anticipation of cats than dogs may be because it is true that dogs have owners while cats have staff—and cats always expect their staff to be readily available to respond to their needs. That does seem to be Tinkerbell's attitude in my experience.

50. In this survey the *least* responsive dogs were Labrador retrievers and German shepherds, both with a 38 percent responsiveness rate. This result again is not statistically significantly different from the average of about 50 percent for all dogs.

51. Sheldrake, R. (2011). *Dogs That Know When Their Owners Are Coming Home and Other Unexplained Powers of Animals*, 2nd ed. New York, NY: Crown Publishing Group. See particularly pages 132–33.

52. Sheldrake, R. and Morgana, A. Testing a Language-Using Parrot for Telepathy. *Journal of Scientific Exploration*, 17, 602–15.

53. The remaining ten vocabulary words could not be included because appropriate images of them could not be found.

54. The variation in results depended on exactly how the results were analyzed, for example, whether it included only trials in which N'kisi repeated the target word more than once, or trials including only vocabulary words N'kisi commonly spoke, and so on. The point is, no matter how you interpreted the data from these experiments, N'kisi was clearly doing something extraordinary.

55. Sheldrake, R. (2011). *Dogs That Know When Their Owners Are Coming Home: And Other Unexplained Powers of Animals*, 2nd ed. New York, NY: Crown Publishing Group, 84.

56. If you are at all interested in the possibility of animal telepathy, I urge you to read Sheldrake's book. His writing is compelling, entertaining, and very easy to follow. The details of his book are: Sheldrake, R. (2011). *Dogs That Know When Their Owners Are Coming Home: And Other Unexplained Powers of Animals*, 2nd ed. New York, NY: Crown Publishing Group.

57. I must say, anyone who has to self-declare himself "amazing" seems suspect to me. But that's just me, I guess.

58. Sheldrake, R. (2011). *Dogs That Know When Their Owners Are Coming Home: And Other Unexplained Powers of Animals*, 2nd ed. New York, NY: Crown Publishing Group, 314 15.

59. For more examples of the highly unscientific attacks on Sheldrake's work, it is worthwhile to study the appendix in his book, pages 307–37. He carefully details the types of criticisms he has received. It is instructive to learn of the flat-out fraudulent tactics used by professional "debunkers" to delay the progress of science in order to promote themselves and protect their strongly held belief systems. Although the specifics concern the attacks on Sheldrake's work, the tactics are nearly universal by psychic debunkers and professional skeptics.

Chapter 6: The Sixth Black Swan: Precognition

60. Actually, in some cases, the people hadn't requested healing at all. They were "ringers" who were perfectly healthy, but who had agreed to participate in the experiment. Some of the "people" were also animals—family pets.

61. Yes, it's true. Occasionally, I really do follow instructions, in spite of all rumors to the contrary.

62. See? I do so follow directions!

63. Okay. So I don't *always* follow instructions. So sue me.

64. This possibly excludes bratty siblings who try to get other siblings in trouble by claiming "Mom, he's hitting me!" long before such a thought enters the other child's mind.

65. Please note that I am in no way implying that my healing of Betsy resulted in a significant cure of her cancer or her depression. In fact, I have no idea whether either of those conditions improved beyond the 2-week follow-up report that she sent in. To this day, I have no idea who Betsy is; all I ever knew about

her was her first name and the town she lived in. Clearly, she felt better after those two weeks, but I am perfectly willing to accept that this may have been simply her belief that someone was helping her in that time frame, though she reported that her friends noticed and commented on her apparent improvement in both health and mood. However, her exact description of what I had done to her is the issue in this instance.

66. As another example, I had a very strong memory of author Michael Crichton's death and I found that very sad. He was an author I admired, and some of his books were favorites of mine. Also, he was still fairly young, only sixty-four, making his death all the more shocking to me. Unfortunately, my memory of his death was in spring of 2008. When he actually died in November of that year, I was shocked all over again. I was absolutely convinced he had died six months earlier because I vividly remembered the hubbub and furor in the press, the bookstores doing big features of all his books in memoriam, the retrospectives in the press and on television, all those media things that go along with the death of a famous person. I even remembered talking with friends about his death—conversations that they say never happened. It was very confusing to me.

67. Radin, D. (1997). *The Conscious Universe: The Scientific Truth of Psychic Phenomena*. San Francisco, CA: HarperEdge. See particularly chapter 7, Perception through Time, pp. 111–26.

68. Radin, D. (1997). *The Conscious Universe: The Scientific Truth of Psychic Phenomena*. San Francisco, CA: HarperEdge, 118–24.

69. That's a bit like an American fruitcake. So if J. J. Thomson had been American, we might have had the "fruitcake" model of the atom. Perhaps it's better to experiment with such food than eat it?

70. Just as well. I'm trying to imagine teaching high school kids about the fruitcake model of the atom. Not a pretty thought.

71. Consider the adage about never being able to step into the same river twice. In essence, the act of observing (stepping into the

river) changes the river, so it's a different river when you step into it the second time.

72. When one of my advance readers (one without a physics background) read this description of how quantum mechanics works, she noted that the interpretation implied that either everything exists through all time, or *nothing* exists, and that existence is solely based on the whims of the observer choosing to observe (or not observe). Her response to that thought: "I am the god of quantum mechanics! You no longer exist! *Die you little serf! Bwah-hah-hah-hah!*" I have strange friends. That's why they're friends with me.

73. Information, like travel, is limited by the speed of light, which is about 186,000 miles per second in a vacuum.

74. Unfortunately, that would mean that we wouldn't have anyone to tell about the scandal, so what would be the point?

75. Cramer, J. G. (2006). Reverse Causation and the Transactional Interpretation of Quantum Mechanics. *Frontiers of Time, Retrocausation—Experiment and Theory*, edited by D. P. Sheehan. American Institute of Physics, 20–26.

Chapter 7: The Seventh Black Swan: Survival after Death

76. Yes, my family did go through a nasty period of deaths in a relatively short period of time. In 1968 there were seven members in my family; by 1973 there were only three of us left alive. It was quite a challenging time.

77. Come to think about it, this is also pretty much the attitude of much of the scientific community toward psychic phenomena, too.

78. While the afterlife I have observed isn't exactly like Christian, Jewish, Islamic, Buddhist, or Hindu concepts of the afterlife, it bears similarities to all those. Thus all those belief systems

appear to have significant truths that I can only respect. On a metaphorical basis, they're all true, even if details may vary.

79. Betty, L. S. (2006). Are They Hallucinations or Are They Real? The Spirituality of Deathbed and Near-Death Visions. *Omega*, 53 (1–2), 37–49.

80. There are also a number of reports of people having a deathbed vision of the spirit of someone not known by the dying person to have died. This happens when the vision is of someone very recently dead, perhaps in a very recent accident or illness in which the news of the death has not yet reached the person having the vision. Hundreds of this type of report have been documented.

81. Nearly always, there is a sense of rising upward away from the body; many report hovering near the ceiling and looking down on the body below them with a sympathetic but almost abstract interest.

82. Interestingly, Chris Carter, in his book *Science and the Near-Death Experience* (2010, Rochester, VT: Inner Traditions) notes that the sense of moving through darkness (or a tunnel) toward a bright light is common only in Western near-death experiences; in those from India or other non-Western cultures, this is rare.

83. Carter, C. (2010). *Science and the Near-Death Experience.* Rochester, VT: Inner Traditions.

84. This highly fallacious logic is also commonly used to "debunk" psychic experiences. Yet the fact is just because it's *possible* to fake a psychic experience in no way says anything about whether the experience actually *was* faked. Even if Alex and Bob and Charlie all fake spoon-bending or mind-reading or anything else, it doesn't mean that David or Egbert do. To imply otherwise is an example of grossly inappropriate generalization (and poor logical skills). Unfortunately, it's also ridiculously common in skeptics.

85. Rock, A. J., Beischel, J. (2008). Quantitative Analysis of Research Mediums' Conscious Experiences During a Discarnate Reading

vs. a Control Task: A Pilot Study. *Australian Journal of Parapsychology*, 8 (2) 157–79. See other references by Schwartz, Rock and Beischel from the Reading List for more details of many other experiments.

86. Schwartz, G. (2002). *The Afterlife Experiments: Breakthrough Scientific Evidence of Life After Death*. New York, NY: Pocket Books.

87. Fontana, D. (2008). Disbelief Despite the Evidence. *Shift: At the Frontiers of Consciousness*, Dec. 2007–Feb 2008 (17) 25–29.

88. Unfortunately, this argument does not prevent scientists like Stephen Hawking, Richard Dawkins, and many others from expounding on how science "proves" that souls and psychics are mere delusions.

89. To those who insist that evidence that lacks a theory cannot be considered as valid, I have to ask if gravity only existed after Sir Isaac Newton explicated his theory of gravity. Until the 17th century, did apples fall upward because no such theory existed? Whether we have a coherent theory or not, *the observations are valid.* Only after we have those observations can we begin to construct a theory that explains them. Without the observations of psychic phenomena or the afterlife, there's no reason to build a theory at all.

90. Gary Schwartz, one the finest investigators of mediums today, was originally brought into the field when his partner's beloved father died, and she asked him to investigate whether there was any possibility he had somehow survived death. Schwartz agreed, but only on one condition: that they would never tell *anyone* what they were doing. He feared—quite justifiably—for his professional career if his colleagues had any hint of what he was investigating. Only later, when he started collecting strong, irrefutable evidence of the existence of the afterlife and was conducting detailed, highly controlled studies, did he decide to go public with the investigations.

91. When I was relocating from San Diego to the East a number of years ago, I had to decide exactly where I wanted to move to. Wherever I went would be someplace new to me, so I considered

a lot of factors in choosing my new home. By this time, I had experienced the psychic awakening described in *Suddenly Psychic*. I told my friends I knew better than to even consider many parts of the Deep South, lest I take the risk of being pilloried or burned as a witch. I was at least half serious about that when expressing that concern. Psychics of all sorts are considered demonic by many fundamentalist sects. Even when I lived in San Diego, I had one co-worker tell me that she thought I was "doing the work of Satan" in exploring my psychic skills.

92. This is not entirely the fault of doctors and nurses. Distraught relatives, terribly afraid of death, demand that every possible extreme measure be taken to prolong life, often at the cost of the quality of life of the dying or the ruinous medical bills that will destroy them financially. Our fear of death approaches the level of terror.

Chapter 8: The Eighth Black Swan: Reincarnation

93. In Tink's eyes, she is my Feline Manager and I am her "minion." I am regularly reminded to keep that relationship clear in my mind. She has other minions, too, like her Auntie Caro, who lives four or five miles away and who gives her "world's best brushies," and her Auntie Joyce, who lives in California, too far away for brushies. Still, Tink can call her on the phone and complain bitterly about her poor-quality minion staff. I should also point out that while *I* stay up all day working, doing chores, and so on, *Tink's* exhausting schedule consists of taking an ongoing series of naps, punctuated by occasional bouts of grabbing a bite to eat (prepared by her minion), getting brushed and petted (by her minion), playing with an occasional toy for a few minutes (leaving them out where the minion will put them away), and supervising the birds visiting the feeder on the deck (kept well stocked by her minion). She has a tough life.

94. I should note, however, that at various times my friends have maintained a list as to which of them gets to be reincarnated as

my next cat because then they'd have a life of dutiful minions serving them faithfully. They've even threatened to auction off the top spot on that list on eBay. I heard through the grapevine that at one point the current bid was well into four figures.

95. Orthodox Islam does not believe in reincarnation, but some sects, primarily ones that derive from Shiites, do have such beliefs.

96. Walter, T., Waterhouse, H. (1999). A Very Private Belief: Reincarnation in Contemporary England. *Sociology of Religion*, 60 (2) 187–97.

97. Burris, C. T., Bailey, K. (2009). What Lies Beyond: Theory and Measurement of Afterdeath Beliefs. *International Journal for the Psychology of Religion*, 19 (3) 173–86.

98. Tucker, J. B. (2005). *Life before Life: Children's Memories of Previous Lives*. New York, NY: St. Martin's Griffin, 3–16.

99. Stevenson, I. (1970). Characteristics of Cases of the Reincarnation Type in Turkey and Their Comparison with Cases in Two Other Cultures. *International Journal of Comparative Sociology*, 11 (1) 1–17.

100. Tucker, J. B. (2007). "I've Been Here Before: Children's Reports of Previous Lives." *Shift: At the Frontiers of Consciousness*, December 2007/January 2008 (17) 14–19.

101. Tucker, J. B. (2007). I've Been Here Before: Children's Reports of Previous Lives. *Shift: At the Frontiers of Consciousness*, December 2007/January 2008 (17), 14–19.

102. Stevenson, I. (1970). Characteristics of Cases of the Reincarnation Type in Turkey and Their Comparison with Cases in Two Other Cultures. *International Journal of Comparative Sociology*, 11 (1), 1–17.

103. Keil, J. (2010). A Case of the Reincarnation Type in Turkey Suggesting Strong Paranormal Information Involvements. *Journal of Scientific Exploration*, 24 (1) 71–77.

104. In accordance with the paper that described this specific case, only initials are used to identify people in this account.

105. As was eventually revealed, M.C.'s family in the previous life were not exactly rich, but they were substantially better off financially than M.C.'s current family.

106. The girl P.P. had been shot when she was only fourteen years old.

107. This case is described in both Tucker, J. B. (2007). I've Been Here Before: Children's Reports of Previous Lives. *Shift: At the Frontiers of Consciousness* December 2007/January 2008 (17) 14–19, and Tucker, J. B. (2005). *Life before Life: Children's Memories of Previous Lives*. New York, NY: St. Martin's Griffin, 3–16.

108. Tucker, J. B. (2005). *Life before Life: Children's Memories of Previous Lives*. New York, NY: St. Martin's Griffin, 2.

109. Tucker, J. B. (2005). *Life before Life: Children's Memories of Previous Lives*. New York, NY: St. Martin's Griffin, 2–3.

110. Laszlo, E. (2004). *Science and the Akashic Field: An Integral Theory of Everything.* Rochester, VT: Inner Traditions International.

111. Note that saying that physics is currently incomplete is not the same as saying that "all of physics is wrong." It is *not* necessary to throw the baby out with the bathwater. What is needed is for physics to be extended to encompass and provide explanations for these phenomena.

112. Bache, C. (2006). Reincarnation and the Akashic Field: A Dialogue with Ervin Laszlo. *World Futures: The Journal of General Evolution,* 62 (1/2) 114–26.

113. Bache, C. (2006). Reincarnation and the Akashic Field: A Dialogue with Ervin Laszlo. *World Futures: The Journal of General Evolution,* 62 (1/2), 115.

114. See Sheldrake's excellent books on this subject, including:

Sheldrake, R. (1981). *A New Science of Life.* Los Angeles, CA: J. P. Tarcher.

Sheldrake, R. (1988). *The Presence of the Past.* New York, NY: Vintage.

Sheldrake, R. (1991). *The Rebirth of Nature.* New York, NY: Bantam.

115. Nothing in this is meant to imply a straightforward upward-growth cycle. Nothing in nature is a straight line—especially not anything to do with evolution and growth. We sometimes grow by taking three steps backward as well as taking baby steps forward.

116. I strongly recommend Goswami's books if you are at all scientifically inclined. He is a clear, cogent writer, and his books are, like Sheldrake's, Radin's, and Laszlo's, top favorites on my bookshelf. A couple of titles to get you started:

Goswami, A. (2008). *God Is Not Dead: What Quantum Physics Tells Us about Our Origins and How We Should Live.* Charlottesville, VA: Hampton Roads Publishing.

Goswami, A. (2011). *The Quantum Doctor: A Quantum Physicist Explains the Healing Power of Integral Medicine,* revised ed. Charlottesville, VA: Hampton Roads Publishing.

117. In this context, a mystic may or may not be affiliated with a formal organized religion; a "religionist," in contrast, is more concerned with a religion's organization, their personal power within the organization, and other outward aspects of the religion rather than inner consciousness.

118. Lest you think I'm in some way insulting my mother by even contemplating considering her reincarnation as a cat, let me remind you that when cats were first domesticated by the Egyptians, they were worshipped as gods. They have never forgotten that, even if we have. In Tinkerbell's eyes, being reincarnated as a cat would definitely be an improvement over being human!

Chapter 9: A Bevy of Black Swans

119. You might be surprised to learn that I do get a sprinkling of skeptics in my workshops. Sometimes they're dragged there by friends or family members, and sometimes they come just to prove me wrong.

120. I have found that drawing is a good way to avoid the whole problem of naming things in remote viewing. By focusing on what their perceptions *look like*, they tend to avoid naming things.

121. While I encourage people to take home their souvenirs, not everyone does so. Also, some people bend multiple pieces of cutlery and take home only their favorites. I do gather whatever pieces participants leave behind and add them to my collection.

122. If you have ever tried to locate your cat or dog to take them to the vet, you know how aware your pet is of your intentions. Intentions to take them to the park to play don't result in the dog-under-the-bed syndrome. Intentions to take them to the V-E-T result in a mysteriously disappearing animal.

123. You know, it fascinates me that so often skeptics accuse psychic researchers of using legerdemain in their research, when so many skeptical attacks on that research use that exact strategy. Misleading or outright fraudulent statements; replacing actual protocol with simplified versions that are obvious cheats; personal attacks on the integrity and intelligence of the researcher—these are all grist for the skeptics' mill. Yet none of those actually address the data the researcher produce. It's all smoke and mirrors designed to distract the reader or viewer from realizing that the skeptic has missed the point.

124. Albert Michelson and Edward Morley were at Case Western Reserve University in Cleveland when they made their

measurements. They devised an "interferometer" that split a beam of light into two parts that moved at right angles to each other. Their idea was that the beam that was traveling along the flow of the ether would have a different speed than the beam traveling crosswise to the ether, just as a boat moving downstream is faster than a boat moving across a flowing river. (This was, obviously, almost twenty years before Einstein pointed out that the speed of light in a vacuum is invariant.) When, through a series of mirrors, they collected and compared the two right-angle beams, they expected one beam (they didn't care which initially) would have traveled faster, and thus would be out of phase with the other. This should have set up an interference pattern between the two. Unfortunately, no matter how they oriented the beams, they couldn't make it happen. Light appeared to travel at the same speed in all directions, with or against the flow of the "ether." Their study was published in a paper:

Michelson, A. A., Morley, E. (1887). On the Relative Motion of the Earth and the Luminiferous Ether. *American Journal of Science*, 34 (203), 333–45. Available online at: *http:// www.aip.org/history/exhibits/gap/PDF/michelson.pdf.*

125. The rationale for the existence of the ether was actually quite a good one. It was known by this time that light was a form of electromagnetic wave. The problem is that waves have to have some kind of medium through which they can travel. This medium was assumed to be a nearly undetectable "luminiferous" (light-bearing) ether.

126. No, I'm not kidding. In 1904 J. J. Thomson, an Englishman, had discovered that the atom was not the smallest particle of matter by discovering the electron. He proposed the "plum pudding" model in which the electrons were like little plums in a pudding, scattered randomly throughout the thick batter. I suppose if he had been an American, he'd have proposed the "fruitcake" model or the "chocolate chip cookie" model. Unfortunately for J. J. Thomson, his model lasted less than five years before Rutherford and his researchers blew it away.

127. In case you're wondering, the reason they used a foil of pure gold is that gold can be pounded so thin that it makes a foil only a few atoms thick. Thus, a beam aimed at an extremely thin gold foil would encounter only two or maybe three atoms as it passes through the foil. There are not many materials from which you can create such a thin foil. Gold is the most readily available of those materials.

128. Cassidy, D. C.; Holton, G. J.; Rutherford, F. J. (2002). *Understanding Physics.* Harvard Project Physics Published by Birkhäuser, 632.

Index

About the Author

MAUREEN CAUDILL was trained in physics and received her bachelor's degree from University of Connecticut and master's from Cornell University. A former senior scientist for a major Department of Defense contractor, she holds three patents on esoteric technologies related to ontological searching, document clustering, and ontological parsing techniques. She has written several science books on artificial intelligence, robotics, and neural networks for MIT Press and Oxford University Press, as well as romance novels for various publishers including Bantam Books. Nearly a decade ago, after having no prior psychic experiences, she discovered that psychic skills are available to virtually everyone, which changed her perspective on the fundamental science that defines our world.

Hampton Roads Publishing Company
. . . for the evolving human spirit

Hampton Roads Publishing Company publishes
books on a variety of subjects,
including spirituality, health, and other related topics.

For a copy of our latest trade catalog, call (978) 465-0504 or
visit our distributor's website at *www.redwheelweiser.com.* You
can also sign up for our newsletter and special offers by going
to *www.redwheelweiser.com/newsletter/.*